WORLD FAMOUS
WEIRD NEWS STORIES

WORLD FAMOUS
WEIRD NEWS STORIES

Colin Wilson, Damon Wilson
and Rowan Wilson

Constable & Robinson Ltd
3 The Lanchesters
162 Fulham Palace Road
London W6 9ER

This edition published by Magpie Books,
an imprint of Constable & Robinson Ltd 2005

A copy of the British Library Cataloguing in Publication Data
is available from the British Library.

ISBN 1 84529 024 0

Printed and bound in the EU

Contents

Chapter One

Believe It or Not

Strange Animal Stories

A large accumulation of excreted methane gas in a pig shed near Verona in Italy was ignited by a spark from a fuse box. The resulting explosion destroyed the shed utterly and killed all 500 pigs. A witness said: 'I saw pigs flying through the air, I thought it was Doomsday.'

The Big Issue

In the *Cape Cod Times Restaurant Guide* an establishment called 'The Sea Gull Café' is listed. According to the description, the café features American cuisine, outdoor dining, and an open buffet. It is open all year round. Unfortunately this pleasant eating place is a hoax played upon the paper: the address given is that of the city's rubbish dump.

National Enquirer

The Anderson Hospital and Tumour Institute in Houston, Texas, has cell cultures of over 300 rare animals stored in liquid nitrogen in preparation for the day when gene science will allow them to be cloned into complete specimens.

Daily Courier Democrat

In August 1978 a strange rumour spread through Uganda, at the time ruled by the murderous dictator Idi Amin. According to whispered accounts, a tortoise had wandered into a small Ugandan village and explained to anyone that would listen that it must be taken to the town of Jinja, on the

Weird News Stories

River Nile, near the country's capital Kampala. There, in the presence of the Regional Governor and the Police Commissioner, it would reveal its dark knowledge. The rumours did not reveal the reptile's news, but they did tell of the unfortunate creature's immediate imprisonment: it was not seen again.

This story was widely believed. It was brought to international attention when several departments of the Ugandan government held crisis meetings at which they strenuously denied the existence of the 'politically imprisoned' tortoise. A spokesman commented that the Ugandan populace was 'always drunk with rumours'. But the story would not disappear. Finally Amin himself held a press conference at which he threatened to shoot anyone caught mentioning the animal again.

Guardian

Among the many remedies available to sufferers of insomnia is a book entitled *Count Sheep*. On every page, the book features hundreds of photos of sheep, arranged in columns and rows for easy enumeration. In all, the home edition features 65,000 sheep; a travel edition is available featuring only 28,000.

LA Times

Vampire bats in Texas are being forced to change their diet. The South American, blood-drinkmg bats at the Houston zoological gardens in Texas have had their supply of beef blood ($1.20/gallon) cut off because of the meat shortage.

Curator Richard Quick explained that the meat packing firm that used to provide the bats' liquid diet had recently been forced to close down. Until the crisis is over the bats are being fed on *human* blood discarded by local hospitals.

Sunday Mirror

When BEA helicopter pilot Captain Dick Hensen set down in a field in Maldon, Essex, he paid little attention to a nearby herd of cows. However, when he returned from making a phone call a few minutes later he was horrified to see that the cows had licked most of the paint off the machine. One had even gouged a hole in the perspex cockpit windshield with a questing horn. The helicopter was so badly damaged it had to be taken out of service.

Sunday Express

Farmer Ted Jewell arrived at the slaughterhouse in Eastleigh, Hants, yesterday, only to find that the back of his lorry was completely empty. The eleven-stone pig he had loaded at the start of the journey had completely vanished. He said, 'A pig jumping a over a five-foot tailboard then down six feet onto the road is almost as daft as a pig flying. But that's all that could have happened.'

The People

'This is a very unusual case . . . pigs eating an aeroplane,' remarked the prosecuting council at a recent case at Devizes Crown Court in Wiltshire. In the dock was Wilfred Grist, swineherd at Craymarsh Farm, Seend, which is owned by Mr Sam Cottle. Grist was accused of deliberately letting 968 pigs out of their sty with malicious intent.

The pigs celebrated their new-found freedom by eating most of the fabric off an Auster aeroplane parked nearby. They went on to lunch on two and a half tons of hay, a straw rick, half a ton of cattle food and thirty asbestos sheets. They also uprooted three acres of pasture, damaged four farm gates and killed ten of their own number in fights.

In his defence, Grist claimed that Cottle had hit him. Then, he said the farmer and his brother had forced him into a car saying that they were going to throw him into a slurry pit.

While attempting the enormous project of constructing a dictionary of ancient Sumerian, scholars at the University of Pennsylvania in Philadelphia found that some of the phrases they encountered on ancient tablets remained semantically difficult no matter how they tried to interpret them. Afrer weeks of work one example stubbornly refused to mean anything other than: 'He put a hot fish in her navel.'

Sunday Times

Mr Cottle did not deny the accusation, although he added that he had soon changed his mind . . . He decided that it would be much better to drop Mr Grist into the giant animal-food mixer instead.

Daily Mirror

Snoopy, the philosophical beagle from the Charlie Brown comic strip, may have assumed a more historical, perhaps even religious significance.

Professor Filippo Magi, director of the Vatican's Archaeological Study and Research, reports a strange find at a dig beneath one of Rome's most historic churches: the papal Basilica of St Mary Major. Under the church are the remains of a huge, first-century AD forum, or market, and among the crowded Roman graffiti on its walls is a perfect image of Snoopy the beagle.

Some Rome newspapers are reported to be showing a picture of the famous dog lying on the roof of his kennel thinking: 'Suspirium! Acetate progredi, heu!' (Sigh! The years roll on alas!).

Daily Mail

San Francisco police were recently called in to apprehend a zebra making its escape from the Marine World zoo down a neighbouring six-lane freeway. After a high-speed chase – up to 45 mph – the animal was finally cornered, but if the cops thought that was the end of it they were in for a shock.

The irate zebra kicked in two doors on a squad car, smashed a mudguard, climbed on the bonnet and chewed the steering wheel. It also bit two animal handlers before it could be returned to captivity.

Daily Mail

Mother Nature seems to have given up being subtle in warning us about the looming environmental crisis – from Albany in Jamaica comes a report of a doom-saying goat. Miss Adele Brown and her mother were out collecting pa fruit when they were approached by the animal. It prophesied that unless the Green Party came to power soon the planet's condition would take a drastic turn for the worse.

Much afraid, they asked what they should do. The goat replied: 'There are no limits to creativity and no limits to subversion. Vote for any candidate opposed to the Year 2000 Party.' Then it wandered into the forest.

Brisbane Telegraph

From the recent *Lloyd's List* comes this environmental snippet: 'The average seal rehabilitated after the Exxon Valdez Oil spill had $80,000 spent on it. Two of the most expensive were put back into the bay at a special ceremony. Within two minutes they were both eaten by a killer whale.'

Observer

Detective Constable Bernard Startup, of Linden Avenue, Oldham, was disturbed at 9.30 p.m. on 5 August 1972 by a knock at his door. The man on his step alerted DC Startup to the fact that a huge hairy pig was eating the young fir trees in his garden. As the pair watched, the alarming animal stretched too far in search of food and fell into the fishpond. While it was thus distracted, Startup blocked off the entrance to his garden with his car, and phoned his colleagues. The animal was eventually tranquillized by a vet.

This oddity became a mystery when it was discovered that the 200 lb beast was a wild boar, a species supposedly extinct in Britain for 400 years. The animal was taken to Marwell Zoological Park when no collector or zoo claimed it as their own.

Aldershot News

The death of thousands of goldfish in the ponds of Britain in the spring of 1977 has been attributed to sex-crazed toads. That spring, male toads found themselves in a ten to one majority over female toads. The resulting dearth of breeding partners left the males mating with anything, water-lilies, sticks, and also pets. The grip of a mating male toad is easily sufficient to crush an average goldfish.

Daily Mirror

Drivers on the M6 near Sandbach were surprised to find themselves sharing the road with a sprinting pig. A police car was despatched, but failed to find any trace of the animal on the road. The sighting is made all the more mysterious by the fact that no one in the area had reported losing such an animal.

Daily Express

A magpie living on a golf-course in Aldershot is blamed for the loss of £11 worth of golf balls. The bird had formed the habit of swooping upon the balls as soon as they had landed, then flying off and dropping them over the fence of a nearby high-security aircraft establishment.

Daily Express

A London branch of the National Westminster Bank has been given the task of guarding a highly valuable – perhaps miraculous – fish. The five and a half inch Butterfly fish has Arabic writing on its tall spelling out, 'Divine Universal. There none but God to be worshipped.' (sic)

The fish was purchased in a Dar-Es-Salaam market eight years ago and an expert has said that the writing is natural and definitely not the work of fraudsters.

The quietly portentous creature has been exhibited around the world and is in the Nat West's keeping only until a suitably splendid permanent home can be provided.

London Evening News

Curious Laws and Lawsuits

Two lawyers from Encino, California, were severely reprimanded by a judge for bringing the bar into disrepute. The pair were neighbours, and one sued the other for playing basketball noisily, thus interrupting his naps and lowering the value of his property. The other countersued for general damages on the grounds that his neighbour played loud rock music and had harassed him by filming his basketball games for evidence.

LA Times

The descendants of Jacob DeHaven are suing the US government for 141.6 billion dollars. They claim that this is equivalent, with interest, to the 450,000 dollars that their ancestor lent to the Continental Congress for the purpose of rescuing George Washington's troops at Valley Forge.

LA Daily News

In 1982 John Crumpton IV and Jane Berry robbed a bank in Los Angeles. While trying to escape, Crumpton was shot dead by the police and Berry was shot and seriously wounded. Subsequently, Berry decided that she would sue the police for not having arrested her on a previous warrant, thus indirectly causing her wounding.

LA Daily News

A grocery assistant, Tom Morgan, sued his co-worker, Randy Maresh, for $100,000 on the grounds that he was inflicting severe mental stress. Maresh was, allegedly, assaulting Morgan by farting at him. According to Morgan, Maresh would 'hold it and walk funny to get to me,' before evacuating himself. Maresh's attorney argued that flatulence was a form of free speech, and so covered by the First Amendment. The judge ruled that no law directly covered the subject of flatulence, and threw the case out.

Time

A by-law passed in Cotton Valley, Louisiana, makes it an offence to play tennis while wearing a hat that might startle a timid person.

Tennis Magazine

In 1990, New York State was forced to pass laws to criminalize participation in two new and popular sports: Dwarf-bowling and Dwarf-tossing. In the former, a vertically challenged individual wearing a helmet is strapped to a skateboard and propelled towards an arrangement of pins. In the latter a similar individual, this time harnessed, is thrown at a padded target. It is not known if all concerned were willing participants.

LA Times

City officials of Toccoa, Georgia, have ruled that no public money is to be used as funding for Yoga classes on the grounds that this discipline is a form of Devil-worship.

LA Times

In 1990, the state of California decided that all personalized car number plates featuring racial insults would have to be returned and renumbered in a less offensive manner. Among those recalled were DAGO ESQ, TOP WOPS, 14K WOP, FOXY DAGO and BBOP WOP. When the plates' owners complained, the state was surprised to find that they were nearly all Italian-Americans.

LA Times

A school in Florida has banned its pupils from reading the fairy tale *Snow White* after Christian parents complained of its 'graphic violence'.

Midweek

Aliens, Visitations and Psychic Occurrences

In 1976, on the back wall of Billsdown Hen House near Bournemouth, someone noticed what appeared to be an image of Christ crucified picked out in stains. The *Sunday People* heard the story and ran a feature article on the 'miracle'. They invited readers to examine a photograph of the wall, and then send in drawings of what they thought they saw. The next week some of the entries were printed. They included a jug, a candle, a group of four angels, a scene of rivers and trees, and Christ reclining on a sofa.

Sunday People

A block of flats in Hamilton, New Zealand, was the object of repeated assaults of hurled bottles. Among the projectiles were milk bottles, beer bottles and coffee jars. Despite a police surveillance set up to discover the source of the attacks, some of which lasted up to four hours, they remain a mystery. Maori elders explained the phenomena by saying that the building was erected on sacred land; the spirits of the land were showing that they were offended.

Sunday Express

Mrs Jean Hingley of Rowley Regis in the West Midlands reported a strange visitation to her local police. Answering her back door one night, she was faced with a blinding light. As her eyes became accustomed to it, she saw three figures with corpse-like faces and wings on their backs standing on her doorstep. Astonished and confused, Mrs Hingley entered into a 'close encounter of the third kind' by asking the visitors if they would like some coffee. They refused, but said they would quite like some water. Formalities over, the aliens entered Mrs Hingley's house and enjoyed a glass of cold water. On their way out, they noticed some mince pies and decided to take them with them. They would, they said, be back some time.

Daily Mirror

In July 1979, identical twin sisters Ruth Johnson and Allison Mitchell Erb were reunited. They had been adopted separately in New Hampshire twenty-six years earlier, and had had no contact since that time. Both women were hairdressers. Both had daughters named Kristen. Both had watched a TV programme defending the right of adopted

Visitors from outer space are always news, but these flying saucers
in Brazil 1969 were only clouds

children to identify their families, and as a result each began the search for the other.

Daily Mall

A policeman called to the home of a man in Toledo found the occupant in severe mental distress because of the invisible dwarfs that were overrunning his home. Obligingly, the policeman mediated: 'I told the one dwarf in the kitchen to leave, then went to the cellar to tell the others . . . They didn't put up much resistance and left.' Convinced, the man thanked the policeman profusely. The question is, how did he know that they were gone?

Toledo Blade

A farmer from Tout in France reported to astounded police that a UFO had landed in one of his fields while he was working. A man and a woman, both naked, had jumped out of the vehicle and proceeded to have sex three times. When the farmer tried to approach the copulating couple, he was thrown back by an inexplicable force. After the third time, the pair jumped back into the UFO and flew away.

News of the World

Since 11 January 1976, a mysterious tree stump has been touring Ridgway, Illinois. The 500 lb stump appears in unlikely places, including inside a van and various people's houses. It stays for up to two days then disappears in an equally inexplicable way.

Lebanon Daily News

Bizarre Crimes

A twenty-three-year-old, bespectacled, Schools' Career Adviser named Graham Carter was arrested on 23 June 1977 at Oxford Circus in London. He was accused of being responsible for a wave of 'clothes cutting' incidents. In the areas around Oxford Circus, Green Park and Piccadilly tube stations, over the previous six months, women had been finding that large circles of material had been removed from the back of their skirts with sharp scissors. Often the unfortunate victims went on their way unaware of the crime until either the draught or a considerate passer-by apprised them of their situation. Mr Carter admitted the offences, but while he was in custody a small number of snippings continued to occur. 'There is certainly one other person, if not more, doing this sort of thing,' commented Mr Carter's lawyer.

Daily Express

Rosana Vigil, aged sixty, was attacked by a man in the street in Denver, Colorado. The assailant prised her mouth open and removed her false teeth. Mrs Vigil told the police: 'He

In both 1976 and 1978, British stuntman Eddie Shingler tried to organize his own crucifixion as a spectator event in Nottingham. Witnessing the actual nailing up of Mr Shingler was to cost three pounds whereas just watching him hang there would be a reasonable fifty pence. Both attempts were foiled by the police, who announced that they would arrest anyone trying to nail Mr Shingler to the cross on a charge of assault.

Daily Mirror

Arthur Gloria, a candidate for the Chicago police, was so determined not to let anything go wrong in his entrance test that he stole a car in order to be on time. When he arrived, he parked the car illegally. As he was dragged away by those he so wished to emulate, Gloria commented that he thought he had done well on the test.

Ann Arbor News

said "There aint no gold here, so here's your teeth", and he gave them back.'

New York Post

In Tokyo, a twenty-six-year-old draughtsman was arrested for scratching the faces of twelve women with his tie-pin. He explained that travelling to and from work on crowded tube trains depressed him terribly, and that disfiguring fellow passengers helped him to relax. The man had a history of mental illness.

Straits Times (Singapore)

Mr Michael Douglas-Smith was driving back from a fancy-dress party when he was torn from his car by three large men and shoved into their vehicle. After having driven a few metres with their hostage, who was dressed as a fairy, the men had a change of mind. Mr Douglas-Smith was dumped by the side of the road and the assailants' car sped away.

Subsequently the three men were arrested and charged with assault. One commented: 'There was a bit of confusion.'

Weekend Magazine

In 1976, a man accused of squatting was dismissed from Brighton County Court because he was wearing a battery-operated flashing clown's nose.

Sun

A young police recruit named Paul Williams decided to fake an assault upon himself. To this end, he stabbed himself repeatedly with a penknife and hit himself on the head with a brick.

After leaving hospital, Williams was given an award for his bravery in the 'assault'.

Unfortunately his fraud was detected: the emergency call for help, as well as other false alarms, were traced to his extension at the police station. Asked why he had done all this, he said that he had expected police work to be more exciting than it was.

Sun

Wendy Bergen, an award-winning news journalist for local television in Denver, planned a series of reports unmasking the vicious underground blood-sport rings in the area. The reports were to be big audience winners, broadcast during the station's 'sweeps', were a test week to establish average viewer numbers for the purposes of selling advertising space.

The problem was that, try as she might, Bergen could not find any illegal blood sports taking place in Denver. In desperation she organized one herself, a pit bull terrier fight, and filmed the violent results. Unfortunately for Ms Bergen, the police were aware of her activities, and she now faces up to ten years in prison.

Ann Arbor News

Three pilots for Northwest Airlines were arrested for drunk flying. One of the three, a captain had a blood-alcohol level over three times the legal limit. He argued in his defence that, as a habitual drinker – indeed, an alcoholic – he had to drink far more than other people before he felt any benefit.

LA Times

One night in 1990 a woman of Van Nuys, California, stepped out of her bed and onto something large and apparently asleep on her rug. It turned out to be a burglar, who, overcome by the twenty beers which he had used to fortify his courage, had passed out.

LA Times

A man who had just robbed a petrol station in Taipei, Taiwan, before escaping took the precaution of performing a good luck ritual to prevent his capture: following tradition, he dropped his pants and defecated at the scene of the crime.

Police arrived before the ceremony was complete.

China Post

In 1990, an Iranian student named Mehrdad Dashti took several hostages to protest against harassment by San Francisco police. One of his demands was that the chief of SFPD, Frank Jordan, should expose his genitalia on local television.

LA Times

In 1990 a Domino's Pizza delivery man of Balch Springs, Texas, was robbed by assailants brandishing only a snapping turtle.

LA Daily News

During 1976–7, a phantom spectacles-snatcher operated in South London, around the areas of Croydon and

As the final step towards casting out a demon that had supposedly possessed him, a young man of Arlington, Virginia, was told to bring all his money so that it could be blessed by his unofficial exorcist; unsurprisingly, she disappeared, along with the trusting young man's $16,000.

LA Times

Norwood. The mugger, a man, began by running up to older women in the street and grabbing their glasses before they could get a good look at him. Of course the victims were not able to give a full description to the police. Eventually a crime was witnessed by someone with good eyesight, and a vague description was obtained. From then on the man committed his bizarre crimes with a bag or a cardboard box over his head. By this he apparently hoped to convince the police that he was a totally different madman stealing spectacles.

By 1977 the man was using violence, threatening his victims with a knife and sometimes hitting them on the head. A spokesman for the police said: 'He must have a drawer full of spectacles at home. Heaven only knows what he does with them.'

Daily Mirror

A man killed his friend in a fight in Thomburi, Thailand. The argument had arisen over the well-worn riddle: which came first, the chicken or the egg. The man left alive maintained that it was the chicken.

Sunday Times

Thieves made a lucky – if very slow – getaway from a building site in Lutterworth yesterday. They were stealing a sixteen-ton, bright yellow, very noisy mechanical digger; but apparently nobody saw or heard them escape.

Daily Express

Psychiatrist Oscar Dominguez, forty-five, is facing a twenty-five-year sentence for the murder of a female patient in São Paulo. She was telling him about her sex life when he grabbed a gun and shot her. 'I couldn't take those nutcases any more,' he explained to the court.

Daily Star

On 20 December 1976, a decomposed human right arm and partial rib-cage was found by builders in an attic in Falmouth, Cornwall. Instead of reporting the find to the police, the builders merely left the remains on their scaffolding with a note attached reading: 'In case you need a hand.' The builders sent to take the scaffolding down discovered the grisly present, but they did not report it to the police either. They left it in the road. After five hours a passer-by discovered the limb and, eventually, the police became involved. The arm belonged to a woman and had been neatly sawed from its body. It was also partially mummified and its age (since severance) was guessed to be between 5 and 100 years. Neither the identity of its owner, nor her fate, could be discovered.

West Briton

A woman from Buenos Aires in Argentina succeeded in obtaining a new trial after she had been imprisoned. She had been found guilty of killing a man, dismembering him, and boiling his head. Her new trial was granted on the grounds that her crime had been committed in self-defence.

Daily Express

Mistakes

Tom Field, from Turnditch in Derbyshire, was both baffled and annoyed to receive two £20, fixed penalty tickets for illegally parking a steamroller in Edinburgh last December. Not only has he never owned or driven a steamroller, he has never been to Edinburgh.

Sunday Mail

A woman trying to accompany an elderly relative to the Gatwick Express train from Victoria found that it was not her day. She was forced to park her car illegally in order to get her relative safely onto the train. Luckily, a policeman agreed to watch over the vehicle during the five minutes her mission should take. Unfortunately, when the woman tried to leave the train, the station guard said 'Oh no you don't!' and slammed the door. Stuck with an unwanted two-hour round trip, the woman was faced with another guard demanding a ticket. 'But I don't want to be on this train!' the woman screamed. 'You're bloody lucky I don't give you a £200 fine,' was the caring reply. He then sold her a £28 ticket. On her return to Victoria she found a £30 parking fine on her windscreen and a wheelclamp that would cost £90 to remove, firmly installed. Worse still was the note left by the obliging policeman: 'People like you are the pits of the earth. I put my trust in you and you betrayed that. You are the kind of person that makes our job a nightmare.'

The Big Issue

990 graduates of the Navy's top educational establishment were surprised to learn that, according to their diplomas, they had been attending a Navel Academy.

LA Times

Weird News Stories

In its July 1991 edition, *Gourmet Magazine* published a recipe for mint sugar cookies. One of the ingredients that the magazine suggested was wintergreen oil, a toxin that can induce nausea, vomiting and in some cases death. *Gourmet* was forced to send 750,000 letters in an attempt to corect the error.

Ann Arbor News

Preparations for a ceremony at the public library in San Jose, California, were delayed when it was discovered that a banner that was supposed to read, in the Philippine language, 'You Are Welcome!' actually translated as 'You Are Circumcized!'

Parade Magazine

Freak Occurrences and Accidents

Doug Pitchard, a thirteen-year-old boy from Lenoir, North Carolina, was admitted to hospital for an unusual operation. Doctors removed a fully formed tooth, including root, from his foot, where it had been growing unseen.

Daily Morning News

A man died while fishing on the banks of the Amazon tributary Rio Negro. Having been attacked by enraged bees after accidentally hitting their hive with his rod, he had sought sanctuary in the river, where he was eaten by piranhas.

Daily Telegraph

Thankamma Mathai fell dead during her wedding at Trivandrum, near New Delhi. Doctors examining her body found a snake bite on the back of her neck. They concluded that a snake must have fallen asleep in the bride's artificial hair bun during the previous night and had awoken confused and angry to find itself on the bride's head.

Sunday Express

A tabloid newspaper in the Philippines featured a story about a woman who had given birth to an adult mudfish. The parents of the animal were apparently quite content with this addition to their family; they put it to live in their bath. All seemed idyllic until disaster struck: the mudfish was eaten by the family dog.

LA Times

Between 1983 and 1988, five American servicemen were killed and thirty-nine injured by a hitherto unknown menace: soft drink vending machines. The accidents usually occurred when soldiers attacked the machines, either hoping to get a free drink, or trying to take revenge on the machine for eating their money without delivering the requisite refreshment. In most cases the machine then fell on the assailant.

Defense Week

Two thousand five hundred years ago, Cambyses II of Persia commanded an army of a thousand men into Egypt. They never arrived at their destination. There was no clue as to their fate until 1977, when Egyptian archaeologists digging in the Western Desert near Mount About Ballaasa began uncovering thousands of bones, weapons and Persian amphorae. The archaeologists believe that the army was on its way to the Amon temple at Siwa oasis when they were engulfed by a huge sandstorm.

Sunday Express

Rangers at the Mikumi game reserve in Tanzania have found a real-life Tarzan. After many sightings and several

Weird News Stories

failed attempts at capture, they cornered him in a tree which he had apparently made his home. He seemed unable to talk and only whimpered like a terrified animal when questioned.

It appears that he has survived in the lion-infested park for some time, subsisting on a vegetarian diet of berries and fruit. At present he is being held in a police cell while they attempt to discover his identity.

Sun

Twenty-year-old waitress Pat Yearsley had a persistent itch in her throat. So she tried to scratch it with an eight-inch dinner fork and to her shock swallowed the utensil whole!

Nobody at the Trefeddian Hotel in Lancashire, where she worked, would believe her. 'Everybody thought I was joking. Even the hospital doctors did not believe it at first.' She said later, 'Then they took an X-ray and realized I was not having them on.'

Doctors were forced to operate on Pat to remove the fork and she had to spend eleven days in hospital. Now all she has to remind her of the episode is an eleven-inch scar across her belly; she was not allowed to keep the fork. 'The surgeon wanted to keep it for his private museum. He said he was frightened I might swallow it again.'

Sun

Fourteen-year-old Mark Henderson had a rather shocking awakening yesterday. He yawned and opened his eyes only to find himself forty feet above his backyard, standing on the roof of his Burnley home. Apparently he had sleep-walked in his pyjamas right out of the tiny window of his attic bedroom. He then made his way, still fast asleep, down ten feet of slippery slates to the very edge of the roof. There, luckily, he came to a halt and stood snoozing.

Fortuately, the neighbours spotted him before he awoke

> On 10 August 1972, a 100-ton meteor streaked through the air above Salt Lake City, Utah, at 33,000 mph. The object was observed by a US Air Force satellite: at its nearest point the thirteen-foot-wide rock was only thirty-six miles from striking the Earth's surface. If such a collision had occurred, the explosion would easily have equalled the destructive power of the nuclear weapon that destroyed Hiroshima.
>
> *Time*

and called the emergency services. Firemen arrived just in tiine to rescue him before he caught cold. He was returned to bed shaken, but otherwise unharmed.

Daily Mail

A Finnish vessel bound for London on 6 July reported seeing an aircraft frozen inside an iceberg in Notre Dame Bay, Newfoundland. The hulk carrier *Burney* radioed the disturbing sighting to a lighthouse keeper who passed it on to the authorities.

Canadian armed forces personnel checked their records for any 'Dakota-style' missing aircraft and searched the bay, but on both counts found nothing. They observed that a rapid thaw was taking place at the time and by mid-July the gruesome iceberg was assumed to have melted.

Windsor Star

A real-life story of Goldilocks and the three bears has been reported in former Soviet Yugoslavia. Five-year-old Goranka Cuclic wandered from her home in the village of Vranje and disappeared into the dense forest. Her parents and neighbours searched desperately for her well into the night, lighting their way with burning torches. Yet they could find no trace of the little girl and when some woodcutters told them they had seen bears near by, most gave up hope.

However, farmer Ivan Furian, Goranka's uncle, refused to stop searching and, armed only with a cudgel, pushed deeper into the forest. As in a good fairytale, his optimism was rewarded: he found his niece cold and hungry, but otherwise unharmed.

Back home and feeling much better she told everyone that she had met three bears in the forest after she lost her way . . . 'One was big and fat, and the other two were quite small,' she explained. 'I played in a meadow with the two small ones and shared my biscuits with them. The big one licked my face . . . its tongue tickled. At night I snuggled between the cubs.' The next day she lost them and had to spend a night cold and alone before her uncle found her.

There are quite a few documented cases of lost children being accepted and adopted by wild animals like wolves and bears so the story might not be complete bunkum – it is nice to believe it is true.

Daily Mirror

In 1922, a meteorite was seen to fall near Omsk in Russia. But when scientists tried to determine where the object had landed, they drew a blank. The rock was eventually located by Professor Dravert of the Omsk Mineralogical Institute. A local farmer was using it to weigh down the lid of the barrel in which he fermented his sauerkraut.

Sunday Express

Alexander Mitchell, a fifty-year-old bricklayer from King's Lynn in Norfolk literally laughed himself to death. During an episode of the BBC comedy series 'The Goodies', Mr Mitchell laughed solidly for twenty-five minutes at a particular scene in which two men beat each other with large black puddings. He then slumped over, dead from heart failure. Doctors attributed the death to the fact that Mr Mitchell was laughing strenuously after a heavy meal. Mr Mitchell's widow, Nessie, commented: 'I can still hear him laughing and it's a lovely remembrance. I shall write to The Goodies to thank them for making his last minutes so happy.'

The Times

Peculiar Behaviour

On 25 August 1977, at 10 a.m., an unidentified man entered a petrol station in St Louis, Missouri, and asked the assistant for five dollars in change. He then walked to the drinking fountain and swallowed the money in handfuls, washing it down with gulps of water. After thanking the assistant, he left.

St Louis Post Dispatch

Until 1990 prison inmates in Texas were used as bait for training attack dogs. The practice was only halted after six injured prisoners sued the state. During an investigation, it emerged that the Vice-Chairman of the Texas Board of Criminal Justice was one of the dog-handlers. So enthusiastic was the VC about his 'hobby' that he even had jackets printed for himself and his fellow trainers featuring the slogan: 'The Ultimate Hunt'.

LA Times

An Arizona man decided to demonstrate his courage to his friends by kissing a rattlesnake that they had come across in the wild. The man picked up the snake and planted a kiss on its 'lips'; unsurprisingly, he was bitten, on the tongue, by the shocked beast. In an effort to remove the venom, the

25

An advert for Parker Pens, run in the *Newsweek* and *Time* magazines over past months, has caused something of a controversy in scientific and academic circles. The ad shows a well-manicured hand writing a complex-looking mathematical formula on a restaurant menu (presumably to suggest that Parker pens are the choice of sociable egg-heads).

Very soon the complaints were coming thick and fast. 'We are getting letters from scientists and chemists who say they can't figure out the formula. Or that it is meaningless,' said Gary Moss of the J. Walter Thompson advertising agency, who ran the campaign. In fact it is not meaningless, it's the formula for a martini. Translated it reads: three and half shots of gin, add half a shot of vermouth over four parts of water (taken down to freezing and cubed), then add three revolutions (stirs) . . . and there you go.

Only one person who wrote in had understood the hidden joke, and he was critical as well. He pointed out that it's no martini without an olive!

Milwaukee Journal

man tried a drastic and unorthodox method. He attached his tongue to the battery of his car.

Arizona Republic

In 1990 La Cicciolina, Italy's porn queen turned MP, offered to defuse the increasingly tense situation in the Middle East by having sex with Saddam Hussein. She said: 'I am willing to let him have his way with me if in exchange he frees the hostages.'

LA Times

A department store in Japan will, for the equivalent of about £50, prepare a gourmet carry-out meal for your pet dog. A popular menu consists of premium rare beef, unsalted ham sausages, cheese and white chocolate for dessert.

Wall Street Journal

The city of Concord, New Hampshire, decided to raise some money by selling guns that it had confiscated from criminals. The money thus raised was to be used to buy bullet-proof vests for the local police.

Wall Street Journal

On 22 April 1990, a mass rally to raise awareness of environmental issues was held in New York's Central Park. Fifty sanitation workers had to work all night to remove the 1,543 tons of litter that those attending the rally had dropped.

LA Times

British troops participating in the recent UN actions in the Gulf were forced to wear thick, green camouflage uniforms, obviously unsuited to the desert environment. This was because four years before the British government had sold all the army's desert uniforms to Iraq.

LA Times

The US Army has regulations concerning almost all aspects of a soldier's life. Here are some extracts from those regarding the baking of cookies: 'They shall be wholly intact, free from chips or cracks . . . The cookies shall be

tender and crisp, with an appetizing flavor, free from burnt
or scorched flavor . . . They shall have been uniformly well
baked with a color ranging from not lighter than chip 27885,
or darker than chip 13711 . . . The color comparison shall be
made under sky daylight with objects held in such a way as
to avoid specular reaction.'

Ann Arbor News

A New York company produces a small wooden device for
the use of business managers who wish to say thank you to
their employees. 'The Congratulator' takes the form of a
clip attached to an articulated wooden hand. Employees
lucky enough to be awarded this prize clip the machine
to their shoulder and, by pulling the string, can pat
themselves on the back.

Wall Street Journal

In late 1977 the play-offs to determine who would play
Anatoly Karpov in the Chess Championship of the World
were taking place between Victor Korchnoi and Boris
Spassky. After having lost three games in ten days,
Korchnoi made an extraordinary claim. In front of the
world's media, he alleged that the KGB were beaming him
with microwaves while he was thinking about his moves, to
confuse his thought and affect his play. He supported his
claim by pointing out that Spassky got up and left the stage
after each of his moves, evidently to get out of range.

Daily Mail

During late 1977 the front doors of four old people's
bungalows at Castleton in Derbyshire were pelted with
groceries night after night. Among the curious 'gifts' were
bacon, tomatoes, bread, eggs and black pudding. The
attacks ceased when the police were called in. One of the
bungalows' occupants, Mrs Ethel Bramley said: 'It's unreal,

weird! If people want to give us food why not wrap it up and leave it on the doorstep?'

Guardian

Two women presented themselves at the gaol in the early morning of Monday; their request was that they might be allowed, as a cure for sore necks, to be touched by the convict's hand, after his death by hanging!

West Briton

A doctor in Moscow has devised the ultimate cure for alcoholism. 'I simply inject a special serum into the top of a patient's backbone,' explained Dr Andronov. 'Mixed with alcohol, it causes paralysis – one drink too many and you're a cripple.' He claimed a 100 per cent success rate in the second half of 1992.

Guardian

The public are respectfully informed that Dr Taylor, the well-known water-doctor, from Manchester, who has performed so many cures in this neighbourhood, from the multiplicity of business in the vicinity of Bodmin and Truro, has not been able to attend to the patients as well as he could have wished, which has obliged them to remain all night, to their great inconvenience and additional expense; the doctor has now the pleasure to announce that, for the accommodation of his numerous patients, he will attend at the following places every market-day, where man, woman or child, bringing or sending their morning urine, may be told whether they are curable or not, free of any expense, as he charges nothing for his advice whatever.

Dr Taylor may be consulted at the New Inn, Falmouth, every Tuesday; at the White Hart, Truro, every Wednesday; at the Star Inn, Penzance, every Thursday; at the London

Inn, Redruth, every Friday; and at the Fountain Inn, Liskeard, every Saturday . . .

West Briton

Police investigating strange cries in the night coming from the cemetery of St Mary's Church, Felling, Durham, found a full set of clothes and a pair of false teeth, but no sign of the owner. A senior officer commented: 'There are no reports of anyone looking suspiciously undressed.'

Daily Mirror

An ingenious individual of Liskeard, named Trethake, has for some time past been exhibiting himself to families in that town and neighbourhood, in a dress composed from top to toe of rat's skins, which he has been collecting for three and a half years. The dress was made entirely by himself, and consists of hat, neck-kerchief, coat, waistcoat, trousers, tippet, gaiters and . . . The number of rats whose skins he has thus appropriated is 670, and when he is fully dressed, he appears for all the world like one of the Esquimaux described in the account of Capt. Lyon's voyage; it should be mentioned that the tippet or boa (but not round like that worn by ladies) is composed of the pieces of skin immediately around the tails, and is a very curious part of the dress, containing about 600 tails and those none of the shortest.

West Briton

Geoffrey Wilson, eighteen, made a gruesome discovery while inspecting the roof of his East London home yesterday. Checking for damage after heavy rain, he happened to glance into his upstairs neighbour's window and saw a fully dressed skeleton lying on the bed. The police were called and identified the corpse as William Blackhally, the husband of the upstairs tenant. →cont.

Henri Rochatain, the man who walked 4,000 miles around France on a pair of stilts, has pulled off an even more amazing feat: for the last six months he has been living on a tightrope – literally.

For half a year he has eaten, exercised and even slept on a stretch of rope suspended eighty-two feet above a supermarket car park in St Etienne, France, without once coming down. His only articles of furniture were a covered toilet and a board bed. These were not attached to anything; while in use they were simply balanced on the rope. He had no defence against the elements and lived on a diet of seaweed soup, biscuits and tea.

Scientists were amazed by his endurance. 'It is fantastic that he managed to sleep at all,' said Dr Paul Monet, whose team monitored Rochatain's nervous system through electrodes attached to his skin. 'He slept well even in thunderstorms and high winds. It is quite astonishing that he could rest, knowing that if he turned over in the night he would plunge off the rope.'

M. Rochatain passed the time by walking up and down, doing stunts like standing on his head and occasionally pretending to fall off. He was not just in it for the thrills and the scientific discovery though. The owner of the supermarket over which he was perched paid him a large fee for attracting so many onlookers/customers.

Daily Mail

Weird News Stories

Neighbours had noted that he had gone missing about ten years ago, but had assumed that he had left his spouse. In fact he had died of natural causes and she had simply left him where he was. Mrs Blackhally is receiving medical attention.

Daily Express

Family planners in South Australia recently hit on what seemed an excellent idea to help teach Aboriginal women about contraception. Since songs and singing are an essential part of the Aboriginal culture they composed a song full of helpful hints about avoiding pregnancy and taught it to the locals.

As they had hoped, the song had soon been spread near and far, but unfortunately something had been lost in the retelling. Many women were apparently under the impression that the song itself was all they needed to stop pregnancy.

Sunday Mirror

Many adults still have the teddy or doll that they had when they were children, but Harriet Lasky of Denver, Colorado, has something a little more idiosyncratic: she has kept the same piece of bubble gum for thirty-three years. Since she was seven years old she has been munching the gum by day and keeping it in a glass of water at night. 'It gets better with age,' she commented.

Sunday Mail

In July 1974, Chris Chubbock, a presenter on 'Sarasota Digest', a local TV news programme on Florida's Channel 40, attempted suicide on air. During an unscripted apology for technical difficulties, Chubbock announced: 'In keeping with Channel 40's policy of bringing the latest news in living colour, you are going to see another first: attempted suicide.' She then produced a .38 revolver from below the desk aimed it at the back of her head and fired. A spokesman for the station commented that the attempt must have been planned, as Chubbock had left a script on her desk containing an item detailing her suicide to be used in the show. At the time of the report Chubbock was not expected to survive.

Sun

On Friday last, the people assembled at St Austell market were surprised by the appearance of a man of advanced age leading a woman of about thirty, by a halter which was tied round her waist. The fellow is named George Trethewey, a labourer residing in the parish of St Stephens, in Branwell, and having become tired of his wife, he adopted this mode of leading her into the market, in order to dispose of her to the best bidder . . . Amongst those assembled were two itinerant tinkers, who travel in company; one of them offered two pence for the woman, and after some time his companion doubled the sum, stating they were acting in partnership. The husband agreed to accept the last offer, when four-pence was handed to him, and the woman delivered to her purchaser with whom she proceeded to a neighbouring pot-house, where they regaled themselves with a jug of ale. Meantime the collector of the market-tolls applied to the husband for a penny; the sum usually demanded for selling a pig, etc. This was at once paid . . .

Trethewey then proceeded to select a replacement for his wife, and after a violent struggle with a man who laid prior claim to the woman chosen, made off with his new acquisition.

West Briton

Hoaxers created new circles during the night, while scientists had
their equipment trained on the area

A Scientific Experiment

A remarkable experiment took place at the Scaramanga
naval base, near Athens, yesterday. Its purpose was to
discover if a legend over two thousand years old might, in
fact, be true.

Some time between 215 BC and 212 BC, the ancient Greek
mathematician and inventor Archimedes is said to have
destroyed the Roman fleet that was besieging Syracuse by
using a 'burning mirror'. The tale is recorded in detail in
Anthemius's sixteenth-century *Remarkable Devices* and there
are also references in Polybius, Plutarch and Lucian's
Hippias, but until now there has been no other evidence to
support its actuality.

Dr Ioannis Sakkas has long held an interest in the fable
and set about devising how the sage might have made a

primitive laser with the technology of the time. 'Archimedes may have employed flat bronze mirrors, the size of large shields, from the walls of the city to concentrate the solar energy and set the galleys on fire,' Dr Sakkas said. 'The flat mirrors are, for this purpose, the most practical as they can be handled by men obeying commands. You can visualize the scene: the Roman ships would hold as they converged on the sixty-foot-high walls of Syracuse within bowshot. The element of surprise was probably crucial, since the target had to be static. The defenders with their shield-like mirrors would focus the reflection of the sun on each galley and set it on fire in seconds.'

At the Scaramanga naval base, Dr Sakkas used fifty or sixty sailors to wield mirrors made of bronze-coated glass, each measuring five feet by three feet. The men stood in a line along a narrow pier 130 feet from the target and moved their mirrors as ordered. The target was a six-foot rowing boat with an outline of a galley made of tarred plywood – a slow-burning material – attached to the landward side. 'The reflective power would be about one-tenth less than the polished bronze Archimedes would have used, and the sun today is fairly weak,' explained the doctor. Nevertheless, once all the mirrors were beaming at it, the galley cut-out was burning after only two minutes. 'The heat generated today must have ranged between 280 and 340 degrees centigrade,' estimated Dr Sakkas.

The Times

Chapter Two

Odd Facts

The term 'skid row' was first used in the lumberjacking days in Seattle. The logs were sent from a hilltop down a long chute and into the sea. Around the lower end of this chute there was a slum area where drunks and down-and-outs often slept in the gutter. This area became known as 'skid row' after the logs that skidded down the chute.

Until the 1930s, no one knew why the sun shines. It was only then that it was understood that it is a vast nuclear furnace.

A cubic mile of sea water holds 150 million tons of minerals.

Benjamin Franklin suggested that clocks should be moved forward in spring to save daylight hours. He died in 1790, but his idea was not adopted in America and Europe until World War I, to save electricity.

In 230 BC, the Greek philosopher Eratosthenes worked out the size of the earth. He heard that the whole sun was reflected in the bottom of a deep well in Syene (now Aswan) at midday every midsummer, implying that the sun was directly overhead at that time and therefore that objects would cast no shadow. At midday on the summer solstice he measured the length of the shadow of a tower in Alexandria, whose height he knew. He also knew that the exact distance from Syene to Alexandria was 500 miles,

George Asher of Joplin, Missouri, was obsessed by horses, which he felt to be superior to human beings. He had his hair cut like a mane, had his shoes shod with horseshoes, and had a harness made with which he pulled a wagon. In his prime he entered competitions against horses to prove he could pull heavier weights. He ate grass, beans, hay, bran and oats – although he supplemented this diet with other food. Asher died penniless in 1928.

having paid to have it paced out. With these figures in hand, he was able, by simple trigonometry to find out how much the earth curved in 500 miles, and therefore how much it would need to curve through a full cirde, 360 degrees.

He calculated that the earth must be 24,000 miles in circumference – only 860 miles short of the true distance.

Mary Shelley's novel *Frankenstein*, written in 1816, was based on a real scientist, Andrew Crosse, whose lectures on electricity were attended by the poet Shelley and his wife in 1814. But twenty-one years after the novel was written, Crosse suddenly achieved notoriety when he announced that he had actually created life in his laboratory. In 1837, he decided to try and make crystals of natural glass; he made glass out of ground flint and potassium carbonate, and dissolved it in sulphuric acid. He then allowed the mixture to drip through a piece of porous iron oxide from Mount Vesuvius which was 'electrified' by a battery. After two weeks, tiny white nipples began to grow out of the stone, and these turned into hairy legs. When he noticed that they were moving he examined them through a microscope and saw what appeared to be tiny bugs. He thought there might be tiny insect eggs in the porous stone, so he sealed his carefully sterilized mixture into an airtight retort and passed electricity through it. In a few months, he again had tiny 'bugs'. A paper on his 'discovery', read to the London Electrical Society, caused him to be violently denounced by clergymen as a blasphemer. Meanwhile the great Michael Faraday repeated Crosse's experiments and obtained the same 'bugs'. Crosse withdrew and led a hermit-like existence until his death in 1855. The mystery of the 'bugs' has never been solved.

What has become known in zoology as 'the Coolidge effect' – the fact that animals lose interest in females after sexual intercourse, but can be stimulated almost indefinitely by a variety of partners – was named after American president Calvin Coolidge. Coolidge and his wife were inspecting a government chicken farm, and were taken on separate tours. As she passed the chicken pen, Mrs Coolidge asked the man in charge if the rooster copulated more than once a day. 'Dozens of times,' replied the man. 'Tell that to the President,' said Mrs Coolidge. When President Coolidge visited the pen, the man passed on the message. 'And does the rooster always choose the same hen,' asked the President. 'Oh no – a different one each time.' 'Tell that to Mrs Coolidge,' said the President.

The camel has never been 'domesticated', in the sense of being friendly to man. It remains a sullen and aggressive creature.

The most literate people in the world are Icelanders, who read more books per capita than any other nation.

The first piece of science fiction was Kepler's story 'Somnium', published after his death in 1630. Cyrano de

Weird News Stories

Bergerac's *Voyage to the Moon* (published 1657), often cited as the first work of science fiction, is not only later, but fails to qualify because it is political satire rather than science fiction.

The first 'best-selling' novel was Samuel Richardson's *Pamela, or Virtue Rewarded* (1740), which went into edition after edition, and was translated into most European languages. Rousseau's *La Nouvelle Heloise* (1760) surpassed it; it was so popular that lending libraries would lend it out by the hour. The first American best-seller was *Charlotte Temple* (1791) by an Englishwoman, Susanna Haswell Rowson, a melodramatic and badly written book that nevertheless went through 200 editions.

The word 'gat' – American slang for a gun – was derived from the Gatling gun, the world's first machine-gun, which was invented during the American Civil War by Richard Jordan Gatling.

The practice of tapping a patient's chest was invented by an Austrian doctor, Leopold Auenbrugger, who used to watch his father – a wine manufacturer – tapping wine barrels to find out how full they were. Although he published the idea in 1761, it was ignored until his book was translated into French in 1808.

There were more opium addicts in America – per head of population – in 1865 than there are today. During the Civil War, opium was used as an anaesthetic during operations, and created 100,000 addicts in a population of 40 million. Today, with a population of 200 million, there are about 300,000 addicts.

The invention of transparent sticky tape was delayed for a

In the early days of World War I, French airmen
carried bags of bricks in their planes. Machine-guns
were not then in use, since the problem of firing
through the propeller had not yet been solved. The
French tried to bring down German planes by
throwing bricks into their propellers, and two
planes are reported as having been destroyed in
this way.

long time because of unsuccessful attempts to find a way of
preventing the rubber-based gum from sticking to the back
of the tape when it was wound into a roll. Finally, it was
discovered that the experiments had been unnecessary: the
gum has a natural tendency to remain only on one side of
the tape.

Many clams in Australia's coral reef are ten feet long and
weigh more than a ton.

The world hiccup record is held – as far as is known – by
Vera Stong of Tennessee, who hiccupped continuously for
fifty-eight days.

Mother Goose was a real person – the authoress of songs
and jingles published in 1716. Her name was Elizabeth
Foster, and she was born in 1665; she married Isaac Goose
at the age of twenty-eight, and died in Boston – where her
nursery rhymes were published – at the age of ninety-
two.

In 1822, Thomas Dawson, ninety-one, and Michael O'Toole,
eighty-five, engaged in fisticuffs to settle an argument and
'fought to a finish' in Garford, Berks. O'Toole collapsed

first, but ninety-one-year-old Dawson died a few hours later.

The most tremendous contest in the history of wrestling was held between William Muldoon, the 'Solid Man', and Clarence Whistler, the 'Kansas Demon', in New York in 1880. They battled continuously for nine hours and thirty-eight minutes, until each collapsed with exhaustion.

A ton of gold would be worth less at the Equator than at the Poles. At the Equator, the centrifugal force of the Earth's spin, counteracts the force of gravity, and would cause the gold to weigh fractionally less.

All the gold in the world could be placed under the curved base of the Eiffel Tower.

Ladak in Kashmir – high in the Himalayas – has the greatest temperature changes in the world. The temperature can drop from 160 degrees in the daytime to 45 degrees at night, and it is possible to experience a drop of 90 degrees by walking from the sunlight into the shade.

All thoroughbred race horses in the world are descended from three Eastern horses imported into England in the early eighteenth century: the Byerly Turk, the Darley Arabian and the Godolphin Barb. Although 174 sires are mentioned in the first *General Stud Book*, these are the only three whose descent has remained intact.

It is possible to sail 200 miles into the Atlantic and still remain in fresh water, by sailing out from the mouth of the Amazon, which disgorges over a million cubic feet of water a second into the sea. Ships far out at sea used to stock up with fresh water from this current – sometimes two hundred miles from land.

On 13 February 1746, a Frenchman named Jean Marie Dunbarry was hanged for murdering his father. Precisely a century later, on 13 February 1846, another Jean Marie Dunbarry, great-grandson of the other, was also hanged for murdering his father.

Big hailstones fall continually on the active volcano of Colima, in Mexico. The tremendous updraft from the boiling lava carries a column of air upward to cold regions were moisture turns to hail.

Local peasants gather the ice, wrap it in straw, and sell it in the villages.

The coldest place on earth is not the North nor the South Pole, but Verkovank in Siberia, where a temperature of 100½ degrees below zero has been registered. The North Pole is about 60½ below, while the South Pole often reaches 70½ below. North Dakota has also registered 70½ below.

According to *Encyclopaedia Britannica*, mules – the offspring of a horse and a donkey – are sterile. In the 1930s Old Beck, a mule owned by the Texas Agricultural and Mechanical College, proved this wrong by giving birth to two offspring, one sired by a donkey, one by a horse.

Weird News Stories

Waves do not actually travel, in spite of appearances. The water only moves up and down; it is the force that travels. The simplest way to demonstrate this is to throw a stone into a pond with a paper boat in it . . . Although the waves appear to travel outwards, the boat merely bobs up and down.

Albert E. Herpin of Trenton, New Jersey, was a poor sleeper; in fact, he never slept at all during his lifetime. Born with a disorder that prevented him from falling asleep, Herpin lived to a ripe old age working as a gardener; at night, he read newspapers, an average of seven a night.

A man known as 'Old Boots' in Ripon, Yorkshire, who lived in the middle of the eighteenth century, had such an upward curving chin and downward curving nose that he could hold a coin between his nose and chin.

On 5 December 1664, a man named Hugh Williams was the only survivor of a boat that sank crossing the Menai Strait – between Anglesey and Carnarvonshire in Wales. On 5 December 1785, the sole survivor of another such accident was also called Hugh Williams; sixty other passengers were drowned. On 5 August 1820, a man

Oswaldus Norhingerus, who lived in the time of Shakespeare, specialized in carving miniature objects out of ivory. He once carved 16,000 table utensils so small that they could be accommodated in a cup the size of a coffee bean. Each dish was almost invisible to the naked eye, yet perfect in every detail. Pope Paul V viewed them through a powerful pair of spectacles.

The 'Amorique market gardeners', Brittany, France are trying to tap
into the growing market for exotic edible flowers

named Hugh Williams was again the sole survivor out of twenty-six passengers.

Both ice and steam are dry; ice is only wet when it melts, steam only wet when it condenses. Uncondensed steam is also invisible.

Siamese twins named Millie and Christina were famous singers, Millie a soprano and Christina a contralto. Born in Wilmington, North Carolina, in 1851, the twins had four legs but only one body. Either head could control the other's feet, so Millie could sing while beating time with Christina's foot, and Christina could sing while beating time with Millie's foot. They sang throughout America and Europe, and died in Wilmington in 1911, aged sixty.

Edgar Allan Poe received only $10 for his most famous poem, 'The Raven'. The manuscript was later sold for $200,000.

Alexander the Great, besides Alexandria, also built a city called Bucephala, named after his horse Bucephalus, which was killed in battle in 326 BC.

The largest statue of the Buddha in the world is in Pegu, Burma – it is 180 feet long and is in a reclining position.The statue was lost for 400 years: all records of it vanish around the middle of the fifteenth century, and it was not found again until 1881, when a railway was being built. The statue was covered with earth and vegetation.

There was one queen of England who never even saw her realm. She was the wife of Richard the Lionheart, Queen Berengaria, daughter of Sancho VI of Navarre. They were married in Cyprus in May 1191. The King's wanderings

Francis Bacon was the father of the modern computer: in 1605 he developed a cipher using only *a* and *b* in five letter combinations, each representing a letter of the alphabet, demonstrating that only two signs are required to transmit information. Towards the end of the century, Leibniz developed the principle into the binary system which is the basis of modern computers. 0 and 1 can be combined to express any number.

Bacon died as a result of his passion for experimental science: in order to test the refrigeration of meat, he left his carriage to gather snow to stuff a chicken, and caught pneumonia.

meant that she saw him only twice more; she lived in France and Italy and died in Le Mans, about 1230.

A gravestone in Sarajevo, Bosnia, has been almost entirely digested by human beings. It was believed that the pulverized stone, drunk in milk, would ensure pregnancy, so over the centuries most of the gravestone was chipped away. Finally, it was protected by a fence. The gravestone bears a medieval coat of arms, but the name of the owner has long since been swallowed.

The nearest relative of the elephant is the rock rabbit – the kinship is proved by the similarity of their skeletons. The rock rabbit mows its own hay and lets it dry in the sun, turning it over regularly, and then storing it for the winter.

The misplacing of a comma cost the United States treasury over a million dollars. In the Tariff Act of 1872, 'fruit plants, tropical and semi-tropical' were exempted from tax. A clerk miscopied it: 'fruit, plants tropical and semi-tropical.' Importers contended that this meant that tropical and semi-tropical fruits should be exempted. The treasury disagreed and collected the tax, but finally gave way and refunded over a million dollars. The wording was then changed.

In Montana, snowflakes fifteen inches across and eight inches thick fell during a record snowstorm in the winter of 1887.

Little Jack Horner of the nursery rhyme was a real person. When Henry VIII was preparing to pillage the monasteries, the abbot of Glastonbury sent the title deeds of the abbey to the king hidden in a pie, and carried by Jack Horner. Horner extracted the 'plum' deed of the manor of Mells, which remains in the Horner family.

The word 'dunce' comes from one of the greatest of medieval philosophers, John Duns Scotus, born in 1265. Followers of Duns Scotus, knowns as 'Duns men' or 'dunces', opposed the new learning, and their opponents used the word 'dunce' as a term of opprobrium, meaning someone who lacks learning.

The shrew, the smallest of all mammals, eats four times its own weight in thirty-six hours. It is also held to be the animal from which human beings descended.

Cobra venom is quite harmless to drink.

During the whole time he was world champion, boxer Jack Dempsey fought for only 138 minutes. This was because few opponents survived his savage style of fighting for more than a few minutes. On 8 February 1926, he knocked out four men in one round each, and repeated this stunt again four days later.

In 1644, Danish author Theodore Reinking was given the choice of eating his own book or being executed. King Christian IV of Denmark thought the book too democratic in sentiment. Reinking chose to eat the book torn up in his soup.

The bagpipe was first introduced into Scotland by the ancient Romans.

The average blonde has thinner hairs than redheads and black-haired women. According to the *World Almanac*, the average blonde has 150,000 hairs on her head, while redheads and black-haired women have respectively 30,000 and 110,000.

Chapter Three

The Weird and the Spooky

In the early 1970s, I was co-editor (together with the late Christopher Evans) of a series of volumes called The Unexplained. One of my tasks was to unearth strange tales about ghosts, poltergeists, vampires, werewolves, zombies, UFOs, and various inexplicable psychic occurrences, which could be illustrated by an artist in a double-page spread; the stories themselves were printed in a 'box' in the text. What follows is a brief – and far from complete – selection of these stories.

C.W.

Seeing the Future

At the age of twenty-two the German writer Johann Wolfgang von Goethe had completed his studies in Strasbourg and was about to return home. While in Strasbourg he had fallen in love with the daughter of a pastor in a nearby village. He loved her but didn't want to be tied.

He paid one last visit to his Fredericka before leaving the town. 'When I reached her my hand from my horse, the tears stood in her eyes and I felt sad at heart,' he wrote in his autobiography. Then, as he rode away, he had a strange vision. 'I saw, not with the eyes of the body, but with those of the mind, my own figure coming towards me on horse-back, and on the same road, attired in a suit which I had never worn – pike grey with gold lace. As soon as I shook myself out of this dream the figure had entirely disappeared . . . eight years afterwards, I found myself on the very road, to pay one more visit to Fredericka, in the suit of which I had dreamed.'

Although the phenomenon of seeing one's doppelgänger is traditionally regarded as a death omen, Goethe did not interpret his experience in that way. 'However it may be with matters of this kind generally, this strange illusion in some measure calmed me at the moment of parting.'

Air Marshal Sir Victor Goddard was lost. Flying over Scotland in a Hawker Hart biplane, he was caught in a heavy storm. He needed a familiar landmark to get his bearings, and so flew lower to see if he could sight Drem, an abandoned airfield whose location he knew. He did sight it – but instead of the deserted and dark scene he expected, he saw a busy scene in bright sunlight. Mechanics in blue overalls were hard at work on a group of yellow planes. He wondered that no one paid any attention to his low-flying plane, but, wondering, headed up into the clouds once more and went on towards his final destination.

That was in 1934 when Drem was indeed nothing but a ruin. In 1938, however, the airfield was reopened as an RAF flying school in the face of the war threat. Between these two dates, the colour of British training planes was changed from silver to yellow – a fact that Sir Victor could not have known at the time of his strange experience. Thus, in 1938, anyone flying over Drem would have seen exactly what Sir Victor had seen four years before it happened.

On an April night in 1865 – with the trials of the Civil War still heavy on his mind – President Abraham Lincoln lay asleep and dreaming. In his dream, he was asleep in his huge bed in the White House. Suddenly he was wakened by sobbing. Getting up and following the sound of the weeping, Lincoln found hiinself in the East Room. There he saw people filing past a catafalque guarded by soldiers. The men and women were paying their last respects to a body laid in state.

The face of the corpse was covered from Lincoln's view, but he could see that those present were deeply affected by the person's death. Finally, he went to one of the soldiers and asked who was dead. 'The President,' was the answer. 'He was killed by an assassin.' With that horrifying reply came a loud outcry of grief from the group near the catafalque – and Lincoln woke up.

This troubling dream, which Lincoln told his wife Mary and several of their friends, turned out to be a prophetic one. In that very month, Lincoln went to the theatre for a rare night away from his pressing responsibilities. Awaiting him there instead of a night of pleasure was a fatal bullet from an assassin's gun.

Eva Hellström, a Swedish psychical researcher, once dreamed that she and her husband were flying over Stockholm and saw a traffic accident. She wrote the vivid dream down.

'I looked down and thought we were somewhere in the neighbourhood of the Kungsträdgarden . . . I said to myself, "The green [train] ran into [the tram] from the back . . ." I saw an ordinary blue tram of the Number 4 type, and a green train . . . run into the tram.'

Eva Hellström also made a sketch of the accident as it had appeared in her dream. At the time there were no green railroad cars in service. But when some months later a few green cars were introduced, she was sure her dream was accurate. She then wrote in her diary:

'The accident will happen when the train from Djursholm [a suburb of Stockholm] and the Number 4 trolley meet at Valhallavägen [a Stockholm street]. This is a place where there have been accidents between autos and trains but so far as I know, never with a trolley . . .'

On 4 March 1956, nearly two years after her dream, a collision occurred at Valhallavägen between a Number 4 trolley and a green Djursholm train. The positions of the vehicles were exactly as in Mrs Hellström's sketch.

A foreboding dream saved Lord Dufferin, once the British ambassador to France, from possible death.

His dream was related by Camille Flammarion, French astronomer and psychical researcher.

Lord Dufferin dreamed that he went to the window of his room and looked out, compelled to do so by an over-powering apprehension. On looking down he saw someone walking by and carrying something. The figure looked up, and Lord Dufferin saw a hideous face. At the same moment he realized that the figure was carrying a coffin.

Years later during his service as ambassador, Lord Dufferin attended a public dinner in Paris. A staff member led him to the lift that would take him up to the dining room. When he saw the lift operator's face, Lord Dufferin gasped in alarm. It was the face of his dream.

Instead of getting into the lift, Lord Dufferin went away to try to find out the operator's name. He had not gone far when he heard a crash, followed by screams and moans. The lift had fallen down the shaft. Everyone in it was killed or seriously injured. But the ambassador had been saved by his fear of the face he had seen in his dream.

'I dreamed that I had in my hands a small paper with an order printed in red ink, for the execution of the bearer, a woman . . . The woman appeared to have voluntarily brought the order, and she expressed herself as willing to die, if only I would hold her hand.'

The dreamer, Dr Walter Franklin Prince, was an

American psychical researcher. In his own account of his dream he wrote that the woman was:

> slender of the willowy type, had blonde hair, small girlish features, and was rather pretty. She sat down to die without any appearance of reluctance . . . Then the light went out and it was dark. I could not tell how she was put to death, but soon I felt her hand grip mine . . . and knew that the deed was being done. Then I felt one hand (of mine) on the hair of her head, which was loose and severed from the body, and felt the moisture of blood. Then the fingers of my other hand were caught in her teeth, and the mouth opened and shut several times as the teeth refastened on my hand, and I was filled with the horror of the thought of a severed but living head.

On the night after Dr Prince had his harrowing nightmare, a young mentally disturbed woman left her home on Long Island to pay a visit to her sister. The police later found her body near a Long Island railroad station. Her head had been cut off by a train. Near the body lay a note in which the woman stated that she was seeking decapitation in order to prove a theory that her body and head could live independently of each other. Her name was Sarah *Hand*.

On investigation Dr Prince learned that Sarah Hand, like the woman in his dream, was pretty, slender, and fair.

Bismarck, the Prussian statesman who unified the German states into an empire, fought three major wars to achieve his goal of unification. He became the chancellor of the German empire after the third of these, and King Frederick William IV of Prussia became Emperor Wilhelm I of Germany. Bismarck tells about one of his premonitory dreams of eventual victory in his book *Thoughts and Memories*.

An Abominable Snowman, this picture was taken with a telephoto
lens at a distance of 280 yards, May 1973

In the dream he was riding on a narrow path in the Alps. On the right was a precipice, and on the left was smooth rock. The path got so narrow that his horse refused to go forward any further. Bismarck could neither dismount nor turn around in the space.

In this moment of trial, Bismarck struck the mountainside with his whip, and called upon God. Miraculously, the whip grew in length without end, and the 'rocky wall dropped like a piece of stage scenery'. A broad path opened out, giving a view of hills and forests that looked like the landscape of Bohemia. Prussian troops carrying banners dotted the area. They appeared to be victors of a bloody battle.

Three years later Bismarck was at war with Austria, and his troops marched through Bohemia on the way. They won – as in his dream.

In the third year of World War I on the Somme front, Bavarian and French troops faced each other in trenches across no-man's-land.

One day Corporal Adolf Hitler of the Bavarian Infantry woke suddenly from a fearful dream. In it he had been buried beneath an avalanche of earth and molten iron, and had felt blood coursing down his chest. He found himself lying unharmed in his trench shelter not far from the French front. All was quiet.

Nevertheless his dream worried him. He left the shelter, stepped over the top of the trench, and moved into open country between the armies. A part of his mind told him that he was being stupid because he could be hit by a stray bullet or shrapnel. But he went forward almost against his will.

A sudden burst of gunfire, followed by a loud explosion, made Corporal Hitler fall to the ground. Then he hurried back to the shelter but it was not there. In its place was an immense crater. Everyone in the shelter and that section of the trench had been buried alive. Only he survived.

From that day on, Hitler believed that he had been entrusted with a special mission which promised him a great destiny in world events.

Dr Edmund Waller, an Englishman living in Paris in the early 1900s, was having a sleepless night. He wandered downstairs, and, finding the crystal his father had just bought, gazed idly into it. There, to his surpise, he saw the image of Mme D., whom he had promised to look after during her husband's out-of-town journey.

The next day, Waller again looked into the crystal, and again saw Mme D. – with a man. He rubbed his eyes, and looked once more. The pair remained in view, this time at a racecourse outside Paris. Agitated by all these visions, Waller went to the racecourse the next day – and there met Mme D. with a man whom he took to be the one he had seen in the crystal.

Waller continued to see Mme D., her husband, and the other man in the crystal. One scene showed the illicit lovers in a particular Paris restaurant. On the husband's return, Waller told him about the visions. The two men went to the restaurant revealed by the crystal, and there found Mme D. with her lover.

There was a tragic aftermath to Waller's visions: Mme D. ended in an asylum, a broken woman after her husband had divorced her.

Seeing the Past

Arthur Guirdham is an English psychiatrist. For over forty years he was afflicted by a recurring nightmare in which a tall man approached him.

Then one day in 1962 a woman patient came to see him and descibed a nightmare similar to his own. Dr Guirdham did not tell her of his own dream; but oddly, it never recurred after that. As the woman, whom he calls Mrs Smith, continued treatment she revealed strange facts about her life: her ability to predict the future and her detailed dreams of life in the southern part of France during the Middle Ages as a member of a heretical sect called the Cathars. She did not at first tell the doctor that she immediately recognized him as her lover, Roger de Grisolles, in those dreams.

It is not unusual for a psychiatric patient to have sexual fantasies about the doctor. But Mrs Smith's recollections of medieval France, of the persecutions suffered by her co-religionists, and of being herself burned at the stake were extraordinarily detailed. Guirdham had details from them checked by medieval historians, and the most obscure of them were corroborated. Her memories struck a chord in the doctor's own psyche, and he is now convinced that he too lived as a Cathar in France.

Mrs Dolores Jay is an ordinary American housewife, married to a minister and the mother of four children. But when she is deeply hypnotized, Dolores Jay moves back through time past the time of her childhood and her infancy – deeper and deeper back until she whimpers in German. (When she is conscious, she neither speaks nor understands any German.)

It is 1870. She is Gretchen Gottlieb, a sixteen-year-old Catholic girl, terrified and in hiding from anti-Catholic fanatics in a forest. 'The man made my mother dead,' she says. She complains that her head aches, she talks about a glittering knife, and then, desperately, evades questions. 'Gretchen can't,' she finally wails. And there it ends. Gretchen presumably was killed, and Mrs Jay remembers nothing until her own life began in 1923.

Weird News Stories

Dolores Jay herself can't account for it. She doesn't believe in reincarnation. She has only heard fragments of the taped hypnosis sessions, but she can't understand the language. She has never been to Germany. She has never heard of the little town of Eberswalde where Gretchen says she lived, and which exists in what is now East Germany close to the Polish border. But Eberswalde was the scene of Germany's last stand against the Soviet Union in 1945, and the town was almost completely razed. The records that once might have proved whether or not there was such a person as Gretchen Gottlieb have been destroyed.

Who can explain it? Not the modern middle-aged woman who, under hypnosis, becomes the young nineteenth-century German girl – a girl who remembers her dolls, her home, and her own death.

Tina was born in 1940 in Brazil, but she has clear memories of a previous existence as a child in France and of her own murder by a German soldier early in World War II. She gave an account of her death to the Brazilian Institute for Psychical Research.

'I don't think there was anyone at home that day,' she wrote, 'because it was I who answered the door. It must have been about ten in the morning and the weather was cloudy.' A soldier entered, wearing a round helmet and olive-green uniform. He carried what looked like a rifle and fired it at her heart.

'I remember,' she continued, 'asking for water before I died, but I don't remember if they gave me any. I can see myself lying on the floor on my back, wearing a light dress. I don't remember seeing any blood.'

Tina has had from birth two distinct marks, on the front and back of her left side, precisely where a bullet aimed at the heart would have gone in and out. She has other memories too. In the interval between her death in France and her rebirth in Brazil she was present in the house of her parents-to-be. As soon as she could talk she correctly described all the furnishings in the house before her birth.

Out of the Body

'I neither drink nor take drugs, and all I brought to my bed was a considerable nervous exhaustion which sleep was required to restore.' So begins William Gerhardie's description of his out-of-the-body experience in his semi-autobiographical novel *Resurrection*.

When he became conscious in his astral body he was suspended in midair, light as a feather. Once on his feet he felt as if he were defying gravity. In appearance he

'Having found, Sir, that the City of London should be sadly afflicted with a great plague, and not long after with an exorbitant fire; I framed these two hieroglyphics . . . which in effect have proved very true.' So spoke William Lilly, a seventeenth-century astrologer, suspected of intrigue in the Great Fire of London by a government inquiry committee in 1666. One of the astrologer's 'hieroglyphics' of prophecy is a drawing of Gemini, the sign of the City of London, falling into flames, and it was done fifteen years before the fire that destroyed most of London. According to Lilly's report about the parliamentary committee, he was released with 'great civility'.

seemed identical to his physical body on the bed, to which he was attached by a luminous cable.

When he tried to open the door, he found he could not turn the handle. Then he discovered that he could pass right through the door, and he moved around the apartment, making observations, lit by his own cord.

His new body responded to his thoughts and floated this way and that according to his whims. Part of him wished to fly to distant places, but part was afraid this might sever the link with the sleeping body.

When he awoke, he found that his earlier ideas of life after death had been shattered. It seemed to him that we already have a body stored away, rather like a diver's suit, in our own everyday bodies, 'always at hand in case of death or for special use'.

The biologist and author Lyall Watson was driving with a safari party through the bush of Kenya when suddenly the little bus skidded in the dust and overturned. It rolled over twice and then balanced on the edge of a gully.

A moment later, Watson found himself standing outside the bus looking at it. And yet he could see his own physical body slumped unconscious in the front seat of the bus. A more alarming sight was the head and shoulders, of a young boy who had been pushed through the canvas top of the vehicle when it had come to a stop. If the bus fell into the gully – which seemed likely – the boy would be crushed.

The thought scarcely crossed his mind when Watson found himself regaining consciousness in the front of the bus. He rubbed the red dust from his eyes. The memory of what he had just seen was extraordinarily vivid. At once he climbed through the window of the bus and freed the boy, moments before the vehicle rolled over.

Telling the story in his book *The Romeo Error,* published

in 1974, Watson said 'there is no doubt in my own mind that my vantage point at that moment was detached from my body', but he was unable to provide a scientific explanation for his experience.

The records of the Society for Psychical Research include the following account:

One grey windy day in 1929 a man named Robert went for a swim in the ocean with a friend named Mildred. He had an extraordinary experience, which he related some years later.

The sea was rough that day and the current extremely strong. He was about to head for shore when he heard a faint cry from a frightened youngster clinging desperately to a board. Robert managed to reach him and hoist him onto the board just before he himself was overcome by a mountainous wave. He felt himself sinking.

Suddenly, he found himself high above the water and looking down upon it. The sky, which had been grey and menacing, glowed with a glorious light. Waves of color and music vibrated around him, and he felt an indescribable peace.

Then below him he saw his friend Mildred in a rowboat with two men. Floating near them was a limp and ungainly object that he recognized as his own body. He felt a great sense of relief that he no longer needed it. The men pulled the body out of the water and lifted it into the boat.

The next thing he knew, he was lying on the beach, cold and aching. He later learned that it had taken two hours to revive him. His help had saved the boy from drowning.

Weird News Stories

Few people have had the strange experience of seeing their own body from outside it. One man who did is a British Army colonel. It happened when he was desperately ill with pneumonia. Through the haze of his illness he heard his doctor say there was nothing more that could be done. The colonel, however, promised himself, 'You *shall* get better.' He then felt his body getting heavier and heavier, and suddenly discovered he was sitting on top of the cupboard in the corner of the room. He was watching a nurse tending his own unshaven, apparently unconscious body. The colonel was aware of all the small details of the room. He saw the mirror on the dressing table, the frame of the bed, and his inert body under the bedclothes.

The next thing he remembers he was back in his body, and the nurse was holding his hand and murmuring, 'The crisis has passed.'

During his convalescence he told the nurse what had happened to him, describing the exact motions she had made and the details of the room that had been so clear to him. She suggested that perhaps he had been delirious.

The colonel had a different answer. 'I was dead for that time,' he said.

Among the cases in the records of the Society for Psychical Research is the story of a distinguished Italian engineer. He wrote that one June, studying hard for his examinations, he had fallen into a very deep sleep during which he apparently knocked over his kerosene lamp. Instead of going out, it gave off a dense smoke that filled the room. He gradually became aware that the thinking part of him had become entirely separate from his sleeping physical body. His independent mind recognized that to save his life he should pick up the fallen lamp and open the window. But he could not make his physical body wake up and respond in any way.

64

Then he thought of his mother, asleep in the next room, and he saw her clearly through the wall. He saw her hurriedly get up, go to the window, and throw it open as if carrying out the thought in his mind. He also saw her leave her room and come into his. She came to his body and touched it, and at her touch he was able to rejoin his physical body. He woke up with dry throat, throbbing temples, and a choking feeling.

Later his mother verified that she had opened the window before coming in to him – exactly as he had seen it through a solid wall.

The Living Dead

William Seabrook avidly studied the spirit religions of the West Indies in the 1920s. In his book *The Magic Island* he relates a strange tale told to him by a Haitian farmer. It seems that there was a bumper sugar cane crop in 1918, and labourers were in short supply. One day Joseph, an old headman, appeared leading 'a band of ragged creatures who shuffled along behind him, staring dumbly, like people in a daze'. They were not ordinary labourers. They were zombies – dead men whom Joseph had brought back to life by magic to slave for him in the fields.

Zombies must never taste salt according to the farmer's tale, so Joseph's wife fed them special unseasoned food. But one day she took pity on them and bought them some candy, not knowing it was made of peanuts. As soon as the zombies tasted the salty nuts, they realized they were dead. With a terrible cry they set off for their own village.

Stumbling past living relatives who recognized them in horror, they 'approached the graveyard . . . and rushed among the graves, and each before his own empty grave began clawing at the stones and earth . . . and, as their cold hands touched the earth, they fell and lay there, rotting as carrion'.

In 1837 in Lahore, India [in now Pakistan] the yogi Haridas was buried alive for forty days. British Colonel Sir Claude Wade, Dr Janos Honiborger, and the British Consul at Lahore all solemnly corroborated that he was locked in a box, placed in a sealed pavilion with doors and windows tightly blocked shut, and guarded day and night. After forty days, the box was opened.

Haridas had not gone into the tomb unprepared. For days before his burial he had no food but milk. On the burial day itself he ate nothing, but performed *dhauti* – a yoga purification practice that involves swallowing a long strip of cloth, leaving it in the stomach to soak up bile and other impurities, and then withdrawing it. Haridas then did another cleansing ritual. All the openings of his body were then sealed up with wax, and his tongue was rolled back to seal the entrance to his throat. Then he was buried.

When the box was opened the yogi's assistant washed him with warm water, removed the wax, and rubbed his scalp with warm yeast. He forced his teeth open with a knife, unfolded his tongue, and massaged his body with butter. After half an hour Haridas was up and about.

The Vampire

Do vampires still walk in Romania? In 1974 a gypsy woman told of her father's death when she was a girl. According to custom, she said, the body lay in the house awaiting the ceremonial final dressing by the family. After this ceremony it would be carried to the grave uncovered, so that everyone could see that the man was truly dead.

When the family lifted her father's legs to put them in his burial clothes, the limbs were not stiff. Neither were his arms nor the rest of his body. Rigor mortis had not set in. The family stared horrified at him and at each other, and the fearful whispering began.

The story spread among the villagers – people who remembered, or thought they remembered, the vampires that used to roam in the darkness of night. One unmistakable sign of a vampire is an undecomposed body, kept lifelike by the regular feasting on the blood of the living. Fear licked through the village, and the inhabitants soon came to the house armed with a wooden stake.

The family – bewildered, uncertain, and grief-stricken – fell back. The men tore off the corpse's covering sheet and, in the traditional manner, thrust the stake through the dead man's heart. The vampire – if such it was – was vanquished.

The nineteenth-century diarist Augustus Hare recounts the following story:

> Groglin Grange was an English manor house that overlooked the nearby church in the hollow. It was rented by two brothers and their sister. One night as the sister lay in bed she became uneasily aware of something moving across the lawn towards the house. Mute with horror, she saw a hideous brown figure with flaming eyes approach. It scratched at her window with bony fingers, and one pane fell out. It reached in, unlocked the winlow, and before she could scream, sank its teeth into her throat.
>
> Her brothers were wakened by the commotion, but by the time they reached her room the creature had vanished and the girl lay unconscious and

bleeding. One brother tried to follow the attacker, but lost it.

The girl recovered and bravely insisted on returning to the house. Nearly a year later, she again woke to see the creature scratching at the window. Her brothers, who since the first attack slept armed, came running. They found the creature in flight. One brother fired and hit it, but it escaped into the churchyard. When the two men entered the churchyard vault, they discovered all the coffins broken open except one. In that coffin was the vampire – and it had a bullet wound in its leg.

Ape-man

In 1920 the Polish medium Franek Klusky had a series of sittings with the International Metaphysical Institute, among whose prominent members were the French investigators Professor Charles Richet and Gustave Geley. The seance circle sat with hands linked, and the expert researchers kept the medium under careful observation. Unlike many mediums, Klusky did not go into trance during a seance. He worked in a state of full consciousness, but with deep concentration.

Klusky was noted for a remarkable ability to materialize both humans and animals. His most electrifying seances were those in which strange forms loomed out of the darkness – on one occasion a great hulking creature halfway between human and ape. It was about the stature of a man, but had a simian face, long arms, and hair all over. It smelled, sitters said, like a wet dog. Once the big hairy head leaned heavily on a sitter's shoulder. Another sitter put out a hand, which the creature licked with a large soft tongue.

The scientifically minded sitters called Klusky's materialized ape-man *Pithecanthropus*. Geley believed totally in the medium's psychic powers. On the other hand, British psychic researcher Harry Price doubted his abilities.

Werewolf?

By the admission of William Seabrook who tells the story, it was perfectly true that Nastatia Filipovna was not ordinary. A Russian aristocrat who had fled the revolution, she seemed slightly larger than life. She was tall and powerful with challenging tawny eyes. She had a fearful temper, but also charm when she chose to use it. She didn't like reality – it bored her – but although she fell into a self-induced trance easily, she didn't like that world either.

Then she decided to try the I Ching, the ancient Chinese method of opening the mind to future possibilities. For Nastatia Filipovna it seemed to open a door. 'But it's opening into the outdoors!' she murmured. 'Everything is white – everywhere snow. I am lying in the snow . . . I am lying naked in my fur coat . . . and I am warm.'

She moved restlessly and muttered: 'I'm running lightly like the wind . . . how good the snow smells!' She began to make unhuman sounds, like a wolf baying. Alarmed, her friends tried to rouse her. Her face changed. Her tawny eyes wide open, the wolf-woman sprang straight for a friend's throat. She fell short. Her companions snared her in blankets and held ammonia under her nose. She came out of it.

But Nastatia Filipovna remembered. And she liked it.

Monsters

Late in the eighteenth century a sailing ship off the coast of West Africa found itself becalmed in a placid ocean. The wind had dropped, and Jean-Magnus Dens, the Danish captain, ordered his crew to lower planks off the side from which they could scrape and clean the ship. Three men climbed onto the planks and began their work. They were scraping energetically when suddenly, out of the quiet sea around them, rose an immense octopus or squid. It seized two of the men and pulled them under the water. The third man leaped desperately into the rigging, but a gigantic arm pursued him, getting caught up in the shrouds. The sailor fainted from shock, and his horrified shipmates frantically hacked at the great tentacle, finally chopping it off. Meanwhile, five harpoons were being driven into the body of the beast in the forlorn hope of saving the two who had disappeared. The frightful struggle went on until, one by one, four of the lines broke. The men had to give up the attempt at killing the monster, which sank out of view.

The unconscious sailor, hanging limply in the shrouds, was gently taken down and placed in his bunk. He revived a little, but died in raving madness that night.

From the 1660 report of Captain William Taylor, Master, *British Banner:*

On the 25th of April, in lat. 12 deg. 7 min. 8 sec., and long. 93 deg. 52 min. E., with the sun over the main-yard, felt a strong sensation as if the ship was trembling. Sent the second mate aloft to see what was up. The latter called out to me to go up the fore rigging and look over the bows. I did so, and saw an enormous serpent shaking the bowsprit with his

mouth. It must have been at least about 300 feet long;
was about the circumference of a very wide crinoline
petticoat, with black back, shaggy mane, horn on the
forehead, and large glaring eyes placed rather near
the nose, and jaws about eight feet long. He did not
observe me, and continued shaking the bowsprit and
throwing the sea alongside into a foam until the
former came clear away of the ship. The serpent was
powerful enough, although the ship was carrying all
sail, and going at about ten knots at the time he
attacked us, to stop her way completely. When the
bowsprit, with the jibboom, sails, and rigging, went
by the board, the monster swallowed the fore-
topmast, staysail jib, and flying-jib, with the greatest
apparent ease. He shoved off a little after this, and
returned apparently to scratch himself against the
side of the ship, making a most extraordinary noise,
resembling that on board a steamer when the boilers
are blowing off. The serpent darted off like a flash of
lightning, striking the vessel with its tail, and staving
in all the starboard quarter gallery with its tail. Saw
no more of it.

A Russian hunter in 1918 was exploring the taiga – the
vast forest that covers nearly three million square miles of
Siberia – when he encountered huge tracks in thick layers
of mud by a lake in a clearing. They were about two feet
across and about eighteen inches long, and appeared to be
oval. The stature was obviously four-footed, and had
wandered into the woods. The hunter followed the tracks
curiously, from time to time finding huge heaps of dung
apparently composed of vegetable matter. The tree
branches were broken off about ten feet up as if the
animal's enormous head had forced its way through. For
days he followed the tracks. Then he saw traces of a

second animal, and a trampling of the tracks, as if the two creatures had been excited by the meeting. Then the two went on together.

The hunter followed. Suddenly, one afternoon, he saw them. They were enormous hairy elephants with great white tusks curved upwards. The hair was a dark chestnut colour, very heavy on the hindquarters, but lighter towards the front. The beasts moved very slowly.

The last of the mammoths are believed to have died more than 12,000 years ago, and the hunter knew nothing about them. But did he see mammoths?

In the decade after World War II Slavomir Rawicz, a Polish refugee living in England, wrote about his experiences in *The Long Walk*. In this book he claimed that he and six others escaped from a Siberian prison camp and walked 2,000 miles to freedom. During their gruelling journey to India they crossed the Himalayas. It was there, one day in May 1942, that he said they saw two massive Yeti.

'They were nearly eight feet tall and standing erect,' Rawicz wrote. 'The heads were squarish and . . . the shoulders sloped sharply down to a powerful chest and long arms, the wrists of which reached the knees.' One was slightly larger than the other, and Rawicz and his companions concluded they were a male and female. The unknown creatures looked at the humans, but appeared completely indifferent. Unfortunately, the beasts were in the middle of the most obvious route for the refugees to continue their descent, and the men were disinclined to approach much closer in spite of the apparent lack of interest.

The refugee party finally moved off by another route. Behind them the Yeti watched their retreat with obvious unconcern, and then turned away to look out over the magnificent scenery.

Albert Ostman, a Canadian lumberjack, in 1924 combined a holiday with a bit of gold prospecting. He came near the head of the Toba Inlet opposite Vancouver Island, spent a week exploring, and decided to stop in a lovely glade under some cypress trees. The second night there he awoke to find himself being carried away in his sleeping bag like a sack of potatoes. He saw a huge hand around the partly open neck of the bag.

When Ostman was later dumped out on the ground, he was in the middle of a family of four big-footed monsters – the Sasquatch or Bigfeet. They were all enormous and hairy: father, who had kidnapped him, mother, a nearly adult son, and a younger daughter. The father was eight feet tall, the mother about seven. For six days Ostman was held prisoner, though no harm was done him. He observed that they were vegetarians, eating the grass, roots, and spruce tips gathered mainly by the mother and son. The daughter and father kept an eye on Ostman, but grew increasingly trustful of him. Finally he got the chance to escape.

Fearing to be locked away as a madman, Ostman said nothing publicly about his adventure for many years.

The Poltergeist

The magistrate of Tedworth in Wiltshire, England, could not have imagined the consequences when he confiscated the drum belonging to William Drury – an itinerant musician caught in some shady dealings – and told him to leave the district.

That was in March 1662. Hardly had the culprit left Tedworth when the drum began to produce drumming noises itself. It also flew around Magistrate Mompesson's house, seen by several people besides the magistrate.

After several sleepless nights, he had the drum broken into pieces. Still the drumming continued. Nor was that all. Shoes flew through the air, and chamber pots were emptied onto beds. Children were levitated. A horse's rear leg was forced into its mouth.

The possibility that the exiled drummer had sneaked back and was causing the trouble was fairly well ruled out when it was discovered that he had been arrested for theft in the city of Gloucester and sent to the colonies. The Reverend Joseph Glanville, chaplain to King Charles II, came to Tedworth to investigate the phenomena. He heard the drumming himself, and collected eyewitness reports from the residents. No natural cause was found for the effects, which stopped exactly one year after they had started.

The manager and staff of the Co-operative Stores in the English village of Long Wittenham, Berkshire, were not amused in late 1962 when jam jars, cereal boxes, and other normally stationary objects began flying off the shelves and circling overhead. In fact, one sales assistant fainted. To add to the confusion, the invisible prankster switched the lights on and off. For some mysterious reason, the poltergeist concentrated on the bicarbonate of soda, transferring boxes of the substance from the shelf to the window ledge.

After a week of chaos, the local vicar offered his services and exorcized the shop. The ritual proved effective, and groceries stayed put at last. The exhausted manager and staff set about restoring the stock to order. Despite the apparent success of the exorcizing ceremony, however, they decided to take precautions with the bicarbonate of soda. They put it under lock and key.

This case is one of many in which possible natural causes, such as earth tremors or an underground river, fail to provide a satisfactory explanation for flying objects. If such natural vibrations were responsible, for example, the bicarbonate of soda would hardly have been given such special attention.

The Red Scratch Case

Mr F.G., a travelling salesman from Boston, had returned to his hotel room one afternoon. As he sat working he suddenly became aware of someone in the room. Glancing up he was astounded to see his sister, who had died nine years before. 'I sprang forward in delight, calling her by name,' he said, 'and as I did so, the apparition instantly vanished . . . I was near enough to touch her, had it been a physical possibility . . . She appeared as if alive.' Yet there was one noticeable change in her appearance: her right cheek bore a bright red scratch.

Disturbed by this experience, F.G. went to see his parents with the story. When he mentioned the scratch, his mother was overcome with emotion. She revealed that she had made the scratch accidentally while tending to her daughter's body. Two weeks after this, his mother died peacefully.

Psychical researcher F. W. H. Myers pointed out that the figure was not 'the corpse with the dull mark on which the mother's regretful thoughts might dwell, but . . . the girl in health and happiness, with the symbolic red mark worn simply as a test of identity'. He suggested that the vision was sent by the spirit of the girl to induce her brother to go home and see his mother.

Strange Powers

Wolf Messing was a stage mind reader who fled for his life from Poland to the Soviet Union during World War II. He had been in danger not only because he was a Jew, but also because he had predicted Hitler's death if the German dictator 'turned towards the East'. Hitler, a believer in fortune telling, put a price on Messing's head.

In the USSR Messing faced another dictator's challenge when Joseph Stalin set a test for him. It was not an easy one. Messing was to enter Stalin's country house – a place bristling with guards and secret police – without a pass.

One day as Stalin sat working in the office of his country home, a man walked coolly into the grounds and then into the house. All the guards and servants stood back respectfully as he passed. He walked to the doorway of Stalin's study. When the dictator looked up, he was astonished. The man was Messing!

The celebrated psychic's explanation was this: by mental suggestion he had made the guards think he was Lavrenti Beria, the much-feared head of the secret police at that time. So strong were his powers that, even though Messing looked nothing like Beria, the guards were convinced it was he.

On another occasion, Stalin suggested to Messing that he rob a bank by telepathy.

Messing chose for the experiment a big Moscow bank in which he was not known. He calmly walked in and handed the teller a blank piece of paper torn from a school notebook. He placed his case on the counter, and mentally willed the clerk to give him 100,000 roubles.

The bank clerk looked at the paper, opened the safe, and took out piles of banknotes until he had stacked 100,000 roubles on the counter. He then stuffed the money into the bag. Messing took the case, walked out of the bank, and showed the money to Stalin's two observers to prove his success as a bank robber. He then went back to the clerk and began handing the bundles of banknotes back to him. The teller looked at him, looked at the money, looked at the blank paper – and collapsed on the floor with a heart attack.

Fortunately, Messing reported, the clerk recovered.

José Arigó was a simple man of little education who suddenly began to do skilful surgery in a small town in Brazil. His first operation was witnessed only by the patient. Arigó, who had been in a trance at the time, didn't believe the story himself when told about it. But his second operation took place in public.

It happened when an old woman lay dying, surrounded by her family, friends, and the Catholic priest who had just given her the last sacrament. Arigó was among the friends present. All at once he drew a large kitchen knife and ordered everyone to stand back in a strong German accent and voice that were not his own. He then plunged the knife into the woman's stomach. The onlookers, terrified he had gone mad, stood transfixed. He slashed through the stomach wall, cut out a growth the size of an orange, and closed the incision by pressing the sides of the cut together. The incision closed immediately without a scar. A moment later he was himself again – the plain, somewhat bumbling man his neighbours knew. Arigó had no memory of the episode, though soon the woman who had been on the point of death was walking around the room, recovered.

Dr William Lang died in 1937, but he is practising today in a town just north of London – or so say many who have consulted him. Patients who come to see him meet him in a curtained room. He talks to them, diagnoses the complaint, and then, if necessary, operates on them. Because Dr Lang operates on the spirit body, the patient remains fully clothed. His hands move swiftly and surely, although his eyes are closed, to correct the difficulty in the patient's body – and such correction enables the physical body to function properly.

Patients may have met the medium George Chapman before he went into the trance that allows Dr Lang to appear, but they report that he is quite unlike the formerly well-known surgeon. Dr Lang's voice is a little quavery and high-pitched, and his shoulders are stooped. Those who knew him in life say it is unmistakably Dr Lang.

Patients report that they can feel Dr Lang at work. During the operation his warm friendly manner sometimes grows sharp, and he snaps his fingers peremptorily to indicate which instruments he wants passed by his spirit assistants. Patients say they feel safe in Dr Lang's hands – though the hands are unseen.

St Joseph of Copertino became known as the 'flying monk' because of the way he levitated during ecstatic states. Born Giuseppe Desa in 1603, he was a strange and sickly child. As a teenager with strong religious tendencies – and later as a monk – he tortured himself for penance. But in moments of rapturous joy, usually inspired by religious feeling, Joseph rose in the air with loud shouts and, sometimes, wild movements.

At the age of twenty-two Joseph became a Franciscan monk in the district of Copertino in southern Italy. He became known to the neighbouring people for his kindness and holiness, even though his noisy levitations disturbed his fellow friars. In fact, he was not allowed to join the rest of his brothers in the choir. One day he went away from the others into an obscure corner of the chapel

Father Karl Pazelt, a Jesuit priest, came to the aid of a California couple in 1974 when they were troubled by a poltergeist. The couple, who reported their story to the *San Francisco Examiner* anonymously, believed that it was a devil.

The poltergeist pulled the standard prank of throwing shoes, but also plagued them by setting fires. At one point a plastic wastebasket caught fire and melted. Frightened for the safety of their twenty-year-old son as well as for themselves, they asked Father Pazelt to exorcize the malevolent force. In his opinion this was a case of 'demonic obsession' – that is, the 'devil is *not* in the people, but *around* the people'. According to the couple, the devilish spirit made its presence strongly felt during the exorcism rite 'by knocking both of us down'.

to pray by himself. Suddenly he cried out with special intensity, rose straight up into the air and – to the astonishment of all present – flew to the altar. With another cry, he flew back to his corner in a kneeling position, and then began to whirl around in song and dance.

Joseph was investigated by the Church, but was acquitted of the charge of practising deception by false miracles.

Gerard Croiset Junior, son of the world-famous Dutch psychic who helped police solve many baffling cases, inherited his father's strange powers. He demonstrated this when he assisted in the case of two missing girls in South Carolina – and he did it from thousands of miles

away. It all started when one of the girls' desperate
mother, having heard about the Croisets' miraculous
ability to locate missing persons, wrote to them in
Holland with a plea for help. Croiset Junior replied.

The two teenage girls had gone for a walk on Folly
Beach near Charleston, South Carolina, and they hadn't
been seen since. In his reply to the mother, Croiset drew
a map of Folly Beach – which he had never seen –
including such details as a bus stop and a parked
bulldozer. He also wrote a page and a half of comments.
The accuracy of the map convinced sceptical police to take
him seriously.

In the letter Croiset said: 'The girls will be there [on the
beach], they will be together.' The police found the girls
where Croiset indicated. And they were together – buried
in shallow graves in the sand. They had been murdered.

Two London mediums, Frank Herne and Charles
Williams, were holding a joint seance with a respectable
circle of sitters. The voices of the spirits John King and his
daughter Katie were heard, and Katie was asked to bring
something to the sitters – which she willingly agreed to
do. One sitter perhaps jokingly suggested that Katie
produce Mrs Guppy, a well-known medium of majestic
dimensions. Katie chuckled and said she would. John
King shouted out, 'You can't do it, Katie,' but she
declared 'I will'. The sitters were all laughing when there
came a loud thump on the table, and a couple of people
screamed. Someone lit a match – and there was Mrs
Guppy, her considerable bulk deposited neatly on the
seance table. She was in trance and held a pen and an
account book.

When Mrs Guppy was gently awakened, she was
somewhat upset. The last she remembered she had been
sitting comfortably in her own home – about three miles

away – writing up her accounts. Several sitters escorted the medium to her house, where an anxious friend waited. According to the friend, the two had been in Mrs Guppy's room together when, suddenly, Mrs Guppy was gone 'leaving only a slight haze near the ceiling'.

During the presidency of Abraham Lincoln the vogue for the new Spiritualism was at its height among fashionable people. Even the President – a far from fashionable man – was drawn into it. Colonel Simon F. Kase, a lobbyist who had several times met Lincoln to discuss a railroad project with him, tells of encountering the President at a seance in the home of Mrs Laurie and daughter Mrs Miller. She was known for making a piano beat time on the floor as she played while in trance.

Kase said of the occasion that Mrs Miller began to play, and the front of the piano in truth rose off the floor and beat the time of the tune with heavy thuds. Kase asked if he could sit on the instrument so that he could 'verify to the world that it moved'. The medium composedly answered that he and as many others as wished could sit on the piano. Four men did: Kase, a judge, and two of the soldiers who were accompanying Lincoln. Mrs Miller again began to play and the piano – heedless of its load – began to rise and thump, lifting at least four inches off the floor. Kase concluded ruefully: 'It was too rough riding; we got off while the instrument beat the time until the tune was played out.'

During his investigation of the powers of Eusapia Paladino, the Italian medium noted for highly eventful seances, Professor P. Foa tried to use a photographic plate to register radiations. Eusapia Paladino's spirits apparently resented the interference. As the medium sat in trance outside the curtained cabinet, a hand shot out and tried to snatch the plate. Dr Foa seized the hand as it retreated behind the curtains and felt the fingers, but the hand wriggled loose and hit him squarely.

The spirits then turned their attention to a table, which they sailed over the heads of the company. When the sitter attempted to approach it, the spirits whisked it behind the curtain where it began to break up noisily. Dr Foa saw the table turn over on its side, and one leg snap off. At that point it shot back out of the cabinet and continued to break up noisily under the fascinated gaze of the entire circle. One of the sitters asked for a handshake, and Eusapia Paladino invited him to approach the cabinet. He had hardly reached it when he felt himself attacked by hands and pieces of wood.

The entire circle heard the noises of the blows, and saw the hand moving in the ghostly half-light.

It was evening in Benares, India. The legendary Madame Blavatsky – the small, dumpy Russian mystic and medium with a strangely magnetic personality – was surrounded by several Indian scholars, a German professor of Sanskrit, and her devoted disciple Colonel Olcott.

The professor observed with regret that the Indian sages of old were supposed to have been able to perform amazing feats, such as making roses fall from the sky; but that people said the days of such powers were over. Madame Blavatsky stared at him thoughtfully. 'Oh, they say that, do they?' she demanded. 'They say no one can do it now? Well, I'll show them; and you may tell them from me that if the modern Hindus were less sycophantic to their Western masters, less in love with their vices, and more like their ancestors in many ways, they would not have to make such a humiliating confession, nor get an old Western hippopotamus of a woman to prove the truth of their Shastras!'

She set her lips together firmly, and made a grand imperious sweep of her right hand. With a swish, exactly one dozen roses came cascading down.

Madame Blavatsky returned calmly to her conversation.

Unlike most automatic writers, who received their messages from the spirits, the nineteenth-century British journalist William Stead got messages from the living – and saved them the bother of writing themselves. He would ask mental questions and his hand would write the answers automatically – sometimes he would learn more than the friends wanted him to.

Once he had arranged a lunch engagement with a woman who had been out of town over the weekend. He mentally enquired whether she had returned to London yet, and his hand wrote a long note. It described an unpleasant encounter she had had on the train. According to the message, she had found herself alone in a compartment with a strange man. He came over, sat close to her, and when she tried to push him away, attempted to kiss her. Struggling furiously, she thumped him with his umbrella, which broke. Then the train unexpectedly stopped and the man took flight.

When Stead sent his servant to his friend's house with a note condoling her on the assault, the woman was taken aback. She replied, 'I had decided not to speak of it to anyone.' She added, 'The umbrella was mine, not his.'

UFOs

At 1.15 p.m. on 7 January 1948 the control tower of Godman Air Force Base in Kentucky got a call from the State Highway Patrol. They said that townspeople about eighty miles away had reported seeing a strange aircraft

in the sky. Godman personnel checked and informed the
police that there were no flights in the area. Not long
afterwards, however, the control tower saw the object,
which no one could identify.

About an hour later, three F-51 Mustang fighters on a
training exercise came into view. The Base commander
asked Captain Thomas Mantell, the leader, to investigate
the unknown flying object.

All the Mustang pilots knew that to go beyond 15,000 feet
without oxygen was dangerous. Yet at 2.45 p.m. Mantell told
the control tower that he was going to climb higher to get
closer to the odd craft. When the others reached 15,000 feet,
they could not contact Mantell, who was above them.

At 3 p.m. the control tower lost sight of the weird
aircraft. A few minutes after that Mantell's plane dived,
exploding in midair. The wreckage was found ninety
miles away. The official explanation of Mantell's death
was that he had been chasing Venus. Few believed this
implausible reason – and the mystery remains.

The Stratoliner of the British Overseas Airways
Corporation (now British Airways) was three hours out of
New York on its run to London. At that point, Captain
James H. Howard and his co-pilot noticed some strange
uninvited company three miles off their left side: a large
elongated object and six smaller ones. These UFOs stayed
alongside for about eighty miles.

As the plane neared Goose Bay, Canada, for refuelling,
the large UFO seemed to change shape, and the smaller
ones converged on it. Captain Howard told the Goose Bay
control tower what was happening. Ground control in
turn alerted the USAF, which sent a Sabre fighter to the
scene. When Captain Howard contacted the Sabre pilot,
he said he was coming from twenty miles away.

'At that,' said Captain Howard, 'the small objects

seemed to enter the larger, and then the big one shrank.' He didn't find out what finally occurred because he had to leave Goose Bay on schedule.

These events took place in June 1954. The pilot and co-pilot described the UFOs as spaceships, and were confirmed in this belief by various passengers. However, in a 1968 report by a USAF-sponsored research team, this close-range sighting was dismissed as an 'optical mirage phenomenon'.

As a British steamer ploughed its way through the Persian Gulf near Oman in the summer of 1906, an enormous wheel of light appeared. The vast wheel, seemingly bigger than the ship itself, was revolving in the sky not far above the surface of the water at that point. Vivid shafts of light emitted from the huge wheel and passed right through the steamer. But these beams fortunately did not interfere with the functioning of the boat in any way.

Since 1760 seamen have recounted sightings of unidentified flying objects in the form of a wheel. The Persian Gulf sighting of 1906 was one of eleven recorded reports between 1848 and 1910. Like most of the sea accounts of mysterious luminous wheels, this one remarked on the eerie silence of the phenomenon. Also in common with most other such reports, nothing was said about humans or humanlike beings in the wheels, even though the ascent and descent of these objects were obviously controlled.

Were such glowing wheels in the sky an early and less sophisticated form of flying saucer? Were they operated by beings from other planets who kept themselves hidden or were invisible? Were they just visions of mariners too long at sea? No one has found an answer.

E. A. Bryant, a retired prison officer who lived in south-west

England near Dartmoor prison, was taking a walk on the evening of 24 April 1965. About 5.30 p.m. he arrived and stopped at an especially scenic spot. All at once he saw a flying saucer appear out of thin air about forty yards away. It swung left and right like a clock pendulum before coming to rest and hovering above ground.

Although he was frightened, Bryant was curious enough to overcome his fears and stay to watch. An opening appeared in the side of the spaceship and three figures, dressed in what looked like diving suits, came to it. One beckoned to Bryant, and he approached the strange craft. As he did so, the occupants removed their headgear. He saw that two had fair hair, blue eyes, and exceptionally high foreheads. The third – who was smaller and darker – had ordinary earthly features.

The dark one talked to Bryant in fairly good English. Bryant understood him to say his name was 'Yamski' or something like it, and that he wished 'Des' or 'Los' were there to see him because the latter would understand everything. He also said that he and the others were from the planet Venus. After the UFO took off, some metallic fragments were left on the ground near the place it had been. Later some small pieces of metal were indeed found there.

When Bryant reported his experience, investigators were struck by the fact that George Adamski, author of the best-selling book *Flying Saucers Have Landed*, had died the very day before. His collaborator on this book had been Desmond Leslie. Was there a connection between 'Yamski' and Adamski, and 'Des' or 'Los' and Desmond Leslie?

UFO enthusiasts were startled when the International Flying Saucer Bureau stopped all activity in late 1953. Although less than two years old, the organization founded by Albert K. Bender in Bridgeport, Connecticut, had been prospering. Why did it shut down?

The only person who could answer this question was Bender himself, and he was not talking. Not until seven years later did he talk – and his tale was one of contact with an 'Exalted One' from space.

Bender claimed to have had a direct interview with the Exalted One, who warned him of instant death if he continued to delve into the mystery of UFOs. That's why he disbanded the IFSB. But he learned many interesting things during his interview, and he revealed all when he got the sign he could.

In his interview, for example, Bender asked the space being if his people believed in God. The reply was that they did not, because they did not have the desire to 'worship something' as Earth people do.

Another topic Bender discussed with the space visitor was whether other planets were inhabited. The Exalted One said that there had once been life on Mars, but that it was destroyed by invaders. The Martians had built beautiful cities and developed a vast system of waterways, but had not been as technologically advanced at the time of their end as we now are. Venus was developing life, the being said.

One of the most interesting exchanges between Bender and the Exalted One was about the moon. Bender asked if the Earth people would ever reach the moon, and he was told yes.

Seven years after Bender wrote this, men were indeed walking on the moon.

One of the wildest UFO chases on record took place early in the morning of 1 April 1966. It started when Dale F. Spaur, deputy sheriff of Portage County, Ohio, stopped at a stalled car and spotted the brightly lit flying object that had been reported to his office. He was ordered to follow it. He and an assistant raced after it in their patrol car for about seventy miles, sometimes driving over 100 mph to keep it in their sight.

Forty miles east of the point at which he started, Spaur met Officer Wayne Huston of East Palestine after having talked to him by car radio. This officer saw the flying saucer too, and described it as 'shaped something like an ice cream cone with a sort of partly melted top.' The chase continued into neighbouring Pennsylvania, ending in Conway. Officer Frank Panzanella of that town came to the scene when he saw the other policemen, and told them he had been watching the shining object of the chase for about ten minutes. All four observers then saw the UFO rise straight up left of the moon, and disappear.

The United States Air Force Project Blue Book investigated the Spaur-UFO chase, and labelled it as a sighting of Venus. The four independent observers involved do not believe that was the right conclusion.

Miracles and Other Psychic Phenomena

Josephine Hoare, a healthy girl of twenty-one, had been married for only six months when she developed chronic nephritis, a serious inflammation of the kidneys. Her family was told that she had no more than two years to live. At her mother's suggestion, she was taken to Lourdes.

At the famous French shrine, Josephine braved the icy waters of the spring. Although she felt peaceful, she was not conscious of any change. When she went home, however, her doctor said in amazement that the disorder seemed to have cleared. Her swollen legs returned to normal size, her blood pressure became normal, and her energy increased. But she was warned that pregnancy would certainly cause a relapse.

Several years passed. Then Josephine and her husband had the opportunity to revisit Lourdes, and Josephine lit a candle of thanksgiving. Soon after they got home, she felt a sharp pain in her back. Fearful that nephritis was recurring, she went to her doctor. His diagnosis was simply that she was six months pregnant – and she had had no relapse. Josephine Hoare had her baby, a son, and remained in good health. For her and her family, the spring of Lourdes had produced a double miracle.

In 1933 a six-year-old boy vanished from his home in Miège in the Swiss Alps. After an unsuccessful search for the boy, the town's mayor wrote to Abbé Mermet, who had often assisted police in locating missing people. The Abbé needed an article used by the missing person, a description of the last place he or she was seen, and a map of the surrounding area to do his work. He used a pendulum and a form of dowsing to find the missing person.

After the Abbé applied his pendulum to the problem of the missing boy, he reported that the child had been carried away into the mountains by a large bird of prey, probably an eagle. He also said that the bird – although enormous – had dropped its load twice to rest and regain its strength.

There was no trace of the boy at the first place the Abbé indicated. A recent heavy snowfall prevented a thorough search at the second place, but the conclusion was that Abbé Mermet had made a mistake.

When the snow melted two weeks later, however, a gang of woodcutters found the torn and mangled body of a small boy. It was the missing child. The bird had apparently been prevented from completely savaging the child's body by the sudden heavy storm that had also hidden the forlorn evidence.

Scientific investigation established that the boy's shoes and clothes had not come into contact with the ground where the body was found. He could only have reached the remote spot by air – the pitiful victim of the bird of prey. Later the boy's father apologized to the Abbé for having doubted him.

It was November 1971 in London on a day like any other. In one of the city's underground stations, a train was approaching the platform. Suddenly a young man hurled himself directly into the path of the moving train. The horrified driver slammed on the brakes, certain that there was no way to stop the train before the man was crushed under the wheels. But miraculously the train did stop. The first carriage had to be jacked up to remove the badly injured man, but the wheels had not passed over him and he survived.

The young man turned out to be a gifted architect who was recovering from a nervous breakdown. His amazing rescue from death was based on coincidence. For the investigation of the accident revealed that the train had not stopped because of the driver's hasty braking. Seconds before, acting on an impulse and completely unaware of the man about to throw himself on the tracks, a passenger had pulled down the emergency handle, which automatically applies the brakes of the train. The passenger had no particular reason for doing so. In fact, the Transport Authority considered prosecuting him on the grounds that he had had no reasonable cause for using the emergency system!

Eliphas Lévi, the nineteenth-century writer on theories of magic, seldom practised what he wrote about. But when he was offered a complete magical chamber, he decided to try to evoke Apollonius of Tyana.

Lévi made his circle, kindled the ritual fires, and began reading the evocations of the ritual.

A ghostly figure appeared before the altar. Lévi found himself seized with a great chill. He placed his hand on the pentagram, the five-pointed symbol used to protect magicians against harm. He also pointed his sword at the figure, commanding it mentally to obey and not to alarm him. Something touched the hand holding the sword, and his arm became numb from the elbow down. Lévi realized that the figure objected to the sword, and he lowered it to the ground. At this, a great weakness came over him, and he fainted without having asked his questions.

After his swoon, however, he seemed to have the answers to his unasked questions. He had meant to ask one about the possibility of forgiveness and reconciliation between 'two persons who occupied my thought'. The answer was, 'Dead.'

It was his marriage that was dead. His wife, who had recently left him, never returned.

Chapter Four

Classic One-Liners

W. S. Gilbert said of an acquaintance: 'No one can have a higher opinion of him than I have, and I think he's a dirty little beast.'

Abraham Lincoln remarked of a congressman: 'He can compress the most words into the fewest ideas of anyone I've ever known.'

Lincoln: 'If this is coffee, please bring me some tea; if this is tea, please bring me some coffee.'

Lincoln on General Burnside: 'Only he could snatch a spectacular defeat out of the jaws of victory.'

Franklin D. Roosevelt: 'A radical is a man with both feet firmly planted up the air.'

Humorist Don Marquis on an acquaintance: 'He is so unlucky that he runs into accidents that started out to happen to somebody else.'

Critic James Agate: 'The English instinctively admire a man who has no talent and is modest about it.'

Comedian Fred Allen: 'What's on your mind? – if you'll forgive the overstatement.'

Weird News Stories

> Poisoner William Palmer on the scaffold: 'Are you sure this damn thing's safe?'

The Cynic's Dictionary: 'A pessimist is someone who has to live with an optimist.'

Arthur Beer, to a thin friend: 'How much would you charge to haunt a house?'

Margaret Halsey: 'The English never smash in a face. They merely refrain from asking it to dinner.'

James Barrie: 'There are few more impressive sights in the world than a Scotsman on the make.'

John Buchan: 'An atheist is a man who has no invisible means of support.'

Carlyle: 'Four thousand people cross London Bridge daily, mostly fools.'

G. K. Chesterton: 'The only way of catching a train I've discovered is to miss the train before.'

Oliver Edwards to Dr Johnson: 'I have tried to be a philosopher, but cheerfulness kept breaking in.'

Critic Eugene Field: 'The actor who took the role of the king played it as though he expected someone to play the ace.'

Philip Guedalla: 'History repeats itself; historians repeat each other.'

Howard Hughes, speaking indignantly to a film producer who was asking for more money: 'Eight million dollars is a small fortune!'

Weird News Stories

Austin O'Malley: 'An Irishman can be worried by the consciousness that there is nothing to worry about.'

Rose Macaulay, on a novel: 'It was a book to kill time for those who like it better dead.'

Sidney Smith: 'It was so hot that I found there was nothing for it but to take off my flesh and sit in my bones.'

C. A. Lejeune, film critic, reviewing a film called *Tokyo Rose*: 'No wonder.'

Film critic Hedda Hopper, reviewing another film: 'For the first time in my life I envied my feet – they were asleep.'

Jerome K. Jerome: 'It is always the best policy to speak the truth; unless, of course, you are an exceptionally good liar.'

Arthur Bloch: 'The man who can smile when things go wrong has thought of someone he can blame it on.'

Simon Cameron, American politician: 'An honest politician is one who when he is bought will stay bought.'

Rebecca West on a male acquaintance: 'He is every other inch a gentleman.'

Bernard Shaw: 'The British churchgoer prefers a severe preacher because he thinks a few home truths will do his neighbours no harm.'

Multi-millionaire John Jacob Astor III remarked consolingly: 'A man who has a million dollars is as well off as if he were rich.'

Jack Benny on his reputation for prudence: 'It's absolutely true. I don't want to tell you how much insurance I carry with the Prudential, but all I can say is – when I go, they go.'

Mark Twain: 'The holy passion of friendship is of so sweet and steady and loyal and enduring a nature that it will last through a whole lifetime, if not asked to lend money.'

Mark Twain: 'I have overcome my will-power and taken up smoking again.'

Maurice Chevalier: 'Old age isn't so bad when you consider the alternative.'

Novelist William Dean Howells on guests: 'Some people can stay longer in an hour than other people in a week.'

Sydney Smith, of an irritating acquaintance: 'He deserves to be preached to death by wild curates.'

Chapter Five

Boobs and Misprints

STRIP CLUBS SHOCK: MAGISTRATES MAY ACT ON INDECENT SHOWS

Daily Mirror

The British Prime Minister, Mrs Thatcher, issued a statement from Downing Street saying: 'The IRA are now indiscriminately killing men, women and children, and now they have killed two Australians.'

Sydney Morning Herald

As the war faded and peace loomed, Vera Lynn was able to advise her husband and business manager Harry Lewis that she was going to have a baby. It is a symbolic and logical clinax to five gruelling years as a 'Forces Sweetheart'.

Evening Standard

She said yesterday: 'Julia was born profoundly dead and wears two hearing aids.'

Sunday Telegraph

Heavyweight news on the Oxford Poetry Chair front: W. H. Auden and Cecil Day Lewis, the Poet Laureate, are expected to nominate Roy Fuller, the much respected poet (and solicitor), whose recent slimy volume *New Poems* has been received with something approaching rapture.

The Times

Weird News Stories

Mrs Harrison is friendly, likeable and easy to talk to. She has a fine, fair skin which, she admits ruefully, comes out in a mass of freckles at the first hint of sin. Her husband is away in London from Monday to Thursday most weeks.

Essex County Standard

Mr Ivan Neill (Bailynafeigh) replied favourably to the first question, and on the second said he would use his influence to ensure the preservation of the Lord's Dad.

Belfast Telegraph

The store detective revealed: 'We arrested one woman with a whole salami in her knickers. When asked why, she said she was missing her Italian boyfriend.'

Manchester Evening News

Pinker, a man whose bedside manner is legendary in royal circles, also delivered Prince William and seven other royal babies. They included Londoner Christina Harte, who arrived with a pair of baby shoes tied to green balloons.

Daily Telegraph (Sydney)

Blackburn Times reporter Valerie Seaton will not forget the night she danced with Prime Minister Edward Heath at a Young Conservatives Ball – and ended up in the maternity ward of the local hospital.

UK Press Gazette

Wife beaters form group to help others.

The Press (Christchurch)

Bill Davidson's two children, Kim and Tania, were overjoyed when he came home with a scruffy black and white mongrel from the RSPCA. The newcomer had a touch of whippet, so they called it Streaker.

A few days later, Bill Davidson, of St Saviour's Hill, felt less happy about the new acquisition when Streaker came into the kitchen with a dead rabbit in his mouth. The creature was plump and well-groomed, and was obviously a domestic pet. Tania identified it as the property of her friend Sita Chatterji, who lived next door but one. Fortunately, the Chatterji family was away on holiday in Doncaster. So after dark that evening, Bill Davidson sneaked into their garden and replaced the rabbit in the empty hutch. There were no marks on it, and he hoped they would assume it had died of natural causes.

A week later Bill Davidson saw his friend Varun Chatterji in the local pub and asked after the health of his family. 'They are well. But my daughter Sita is very upset. Her pet rabbit died just before we went on holiday, and some sick bastard has gone and put a dead rabbit in its cage.'

Chronicle (Leicester)

An intensive-care-unit physician at Camperdown Children's Hospital said today that many pregnant children were unaware that iron tablets were lethal to toddlers.

Sunday Territorian (Australia)

Assistant Catering Manager/ess: The applicant would have had experience of managing/working with an extremely busy high-class restaurant/coffee shop with the ability to prepare good food quickly and without taste.

Walton and Weybridge Informer

Warner Lambert today launches a teaser poster for its 'Lifestyle' sheath. Using a new claim, 'The male contraceptive women will prefer', it precedes a major push.

Marketing magazine

'It is quite amazing how much damage and destruction these mindless vandals can cause when they put their minds to it,' said a bitter Mr Rattray last night.

Courier and Advertiser

The MP for west England and Berkeley reckons that a thousand or more Conservatives abstained from voting specifically because of the homosexuality issue.

'I reckoned I was endangering my seat.'

The Times

Did you watch the Olympics last night? If you did, chances are you're not reading this, but taking a well-earned snooze instead.

News (Southampton)

Fortunately for me, at the time when sex was beginning to loom in my life as an enormous and insoluble problem, I began to take an interest in keeping animals.

Armand Denise, *News of the World*

Early in his career as a senator, John F. Kennedy began a speech at a Democratic convention: 'I was almost late here today, but I had a very good taxi driver who brought me through the traffic jam. I was going to give him a very large tip and tell him to vote Democrat, and then I remembered some advice Senator Green had given me. So I gave him no tip at all, and told him to vote Republican.'

Associated Press ran the story, and Kennedy received dozens of angry letters from cab drivers – as a result of which he had to persuade Associated Press to print another story explaining it was supposed to be a joke.

Theodore Sorenson

The Prime Minister: Interviewed by Robin Day on 'Panorama' (8.00, BBC1) . . . Followed on BBC2 by **Heart Attack**.

Observer

Mr Wielden was taken to Warwick Hospital for treatment but escaped serious injury.

Morning News (Leamington Spa)

Miss Morrison, a sociologist and police management researcher at Southclyde University near Glasgow, said she decided to go to Philadelphia because there were sixty-five rapes a month there.

Star (South Africa)

NO WATER – SO FIREMEN IMPROVISED

Liverpool Daily Post

Weird News Stories

Dead-eye Stewart Fraser, who got three against the league of Ireland recently, attempted a shit from twenty yards, but was so wide of the target that he actually found Carlyle with his attempt. The outside-right was so surprised at the 'pass' that he made a mess of his shot at the goal.

Jewish Chronicle

ABATTOIR BULL ESCAPES – ATTACKS VEGETARIAN
Cape Times (South Africa)

Dr Olafson said that while the problem of teenage pregnancy was as acute in Jamaica, in Africa the causes were somewhat different.

Daily Gleaner

Rome, June 20 (AP)
Christian Democrat Senator Giovanni Leone was named as premier-designate Wednesday night and given the task of forming a new government crisis.

Bangkok World

Of the 16 lets bought in 1964, 42 have crashed. 'That's not a bad attrition record,' Public Relations Officer Wing Commander Hancox said.

Midweek Territorian (NT)

Mr Ross George, chairman of a Wellington advertising company involved in producing television commercials, said advertisements may not reflect society exactly but they certainly mirror it.

Auckland Star

Police were searching for a car which failed to stop after a mini-car swerved off the road and crashed into a lamp post at Magdalen Road, Bexhill.

No casualties were reported, but communication or the 135 mile railway – the only link between Addis Ababa and Djibouti – have been disrupted.

Evening Standard

Yesterday it was announced that Cram would run against his Olympic conqueror and former world 1,500 metres record-holder Sebastian Cow this weekend, but Cram said: 'I am going to have to wait to see what sort of reaction I get with my calf.'

Press and Journal (Aberdeen)

There was less weather than usual last month.

Bristol Evening News

Street crime has taken on a new meaning in South Tyneside – where thieves are stripping paths of hundreds of paving stones and gully covers throughout the borough. According to council chiefs, 'The situation has got so bad that some weeks ago we had a whole cul-de-sac stolen from us overnight.'

Journal (Newcastle)

Mushrooms Provençale stuffed with the chef's special recipe and friend in garlic butter.

Blackburn Citizen

The service was attended by Woking mayor John Jewson and the town's MP Cranley Onslow who read the lesson. The Salvation Army band led the procession to the war memorial. Then, as the congregation stood with heads bowed, a lone burglar from the Welsh Guards played the Last Post.

Woking Informer

A parachutist gets tangled in the ropes as he disrupts the fight between Bowe and Holyfield, 1993

Boobs and Misprints

Lost donkey, answers to the name of Harold. Very attractive, dearly beloved by owner. Last seen in a nun's outfit.

Bulletin (Belgium)

President Nixon set off today on a tour of six Asian nations to explain his intentions and assure the countries that he is abandoning them to their enemies.

Daily Mail

A story to make your blood curl.

Stoke-on-Trent Evening Sentinel

Retired doctor Aubrey Westlake is fed up with people asking if his caravan site and holiday centre is a nudist colony.

For 79-year old Dr Westlake and his 71-year old wife cannot understand what makes people think their Sandy Balls holiday centre is for nudists.

Sun

FIVE GIRLS UNDER SIXTEEN HAVE ABORTIONS EVERY DAY

Times Educational Supplement

Princess Anne attended the opening in a stunningly bright peach-coloured kimono-like gown that fittingly suited the evening's Japanese tenor.

Leader Post (Canada)

African grey rabbit, intelligent, tame, very good talker, sold with cage to good home only. First time advertised.

Pershore Admag

Spelling Check-list: A Dictionary for Dyslexics is available from St David's College.

Manchester Evening News

Weird News Stories

Sales experience is desirable but not essential as comprehensive training is given. Starting income negotiable. Male or female preferred.

Crosby Herald

Audrey Hepburn, aged thirty-nine, is to marry Rome psychiatrist Andrea Dotti.

Sunday Times

Toronto lawyer, David Himelfarb, who represented Reynolds, wouldn't comment on this agreement. 'One of the terms of the settlement was that we not release any of the terms of the settlement', he said.

Toronto Sun

Mr Gumo said, however, that the introduction of speed trains would not be an immediate undertaking. 'With speed trains one would arrive at one's destination too early. At the present time you get to your destination just at the right time.'

Nation (Kenya)

Sagittarius: So far as your love life is concerned, this is a time for discretion. Try to create jealousy and bad feeling by thoughtless actions.

Standard (Kenya)

Queen Victoria paid a visit here, but only briefly, and

The court was told that, after the attack, Payne told a VicRail employee that he was God. The employee had then asked for some identification.

Melbourne Sun

> The thieves broke into the centre on Sunday and took 50 dog choker chains and 12 studded leather collars, valued at $366. Police said they were following several leads.
>
> *Dominion* (New Zealand)

because she could not wait until she reached Erlestoke Park six miles on.

Wiltshire Times

6.15 p.m.: Bing Crosby in 'If I Had My Way' with Gloria Jean.

Radio Times

Among the other semitropical guest workers is *Paratrechina longicornis,* also known as the crazy ant. A colony of crazy ants was recently found inside a psychiatric hospital.

New Scientist

Architect with modernized Herefordshire farmhouse and beautiful Hereford cow, seeks similar companion, preferably with a sense of humour.

Youth Hostelling News

The resealing work on Leawood Aqueduct is now complete but unfortunately the Aqueduct is still leaking.

Newark Post

Alleging the issue was stacked, Councillor Malcolm said the council had decided against the toilets prior to the meeting on the issue and 'just went through the motions'?

New Zealand News Advertiser

Weird News Stories

Mr Griffin said last night: 'I am very pleased after this long wait that we are now able to get married. It has been a long time, but was worth every minute. The dispensation had to come from the Pope . . . Both my wife-to-be and myself were and still are active alcoholics, and will continue to be so.'

Yorkshire Post

He followed two girls of 17 in Binney Street and tapped one on the shoulder. The girls turned, gave a scream, and hurried away.

The officer said that he and a colleague ran to the accused and found that he was exposed. Asked what he thought he was doing, he said: 'Nothing, nothing. I was just waiting for my wife.'

Hendon Times

A report in the *Age* on Monday said that up to six million dead had died in a gun battle in Sri Lanka. It should have read up to six militants died in a gun battle. This was a typographical error.

The highlight of the show is Richard Chipperfield's lion act, featuring a group of fourteen tigers.

Southside

Police are baffled as to why a naked woman, aged about fifty, was walking the streets of Pennant Hills early today with a garbage bin on her head. She was taken to Hornsby Hospital and treated for exposure.

Dail Mirror (Sydney)

Give away two kittens, six wks. Will do light mouse duties.
Gold Coast Bulletin

We learn that a tape recording taken in the Legislative

Assembly has now established that the word spoken by Sir Seewoosagur was 'bolshy', and not 'bullshit'.

Once again the Maurician Party has raised a storm in a teacup.

Advance (Mauritius)

Mr Kenneth Aylett, for Dearman, said to the jury that they may find the films 'Dirty, lewd, indecent, shocking, repulsive, revolting, outrageous, utterly disgusting or filthy', but added that those feelings did not mean that the videos were obscene.

Enfield Independent

Borough arts liaison officer Marjorie Farley hopes that the bar, due to open in the next few weeks, together with proposed toilets, will attract a lot more people to Ruislip Halls – both as users and as spectators.

Uxbridge and Hillingdon Gazette

NEWLY WEDS, AGED EIGHTY-TWO, HAVE PROBLEM
West Briton

At a meeting to discuss the route of a proposed ring road, the highways committee chairman said: 'We intend to take the road through the cemetery – provided we can get the permission of the various bodies concerned.'

West London Observer

Situatioin s Vacnat: Focus urgently needs a person to proofread the typed copy each month before it goes into print.

Focus parish magazine (Bolton)

The launching ceremony was carried out by Mrs Lill Bull, wife of Mr Christian R. Bull, and despite her giant size, she moved smoothly into the waiting waters of the Mersey.

Birkenhead News

Don't kill your husband. Let us do it for you. KC Landscaping.

Williamstown Advertiser

Wanted: Babysitter, six months old, shift work, references necessary.

The Star (Qld)

POLICE IN IRELAND HUNT UNWANTED MAN

Oman Observer

Births: Gambardella, nee Bragg – warmest congratulations to Jeannie and Mark and Billy on the birth of their daughter.

Waltham Forest Guardian

Drive carefully in the new year. Remember that nine people out of ten are caused by accidents.

Falkirk Herald

Services: Mini Bouncer for hire; ideal for children's parties, playgroups.

Swift Flash

Business for sale. Urgent. Wagga fruit and vegetable shop with sandwich bar. No goodwill.

Murrumbidgee Irrigator (New South Wales)

Boobs and Misprints

Cecil Jude Lyons, a former St John the Baptist Parish sheriff's deputy who ran for sheriff last fall, died Monday of gunshot wounds inflicted by his wife, who is the parish rabies control olficer, authorities said.

Times-Picayune/States item (USA)

There is a fundamental difference between male and female homosexuality, which is that the former concerns men and the second women.

European Parliament report

Stories about a merger between Coca Cola and Pepsi Cola have been denied by spokesmen from both companies. It had been rumoured that the new advertising slogan would be: 'If you want a new sensation, have a Poke.'

London Business News

According to nature conservationist Mr Tony Joubert, poachers scatter maize pips soaked in pesticide solution near dams and on farmlands. Birds that eat the pips die within a short time, after which they are collected and slaughtered.

Star (Johannesburg)

Five-course dinner menu including a welcoming glass of red wine. Hot smoked mackerel with horseradish and black pepper. Curried eggs (two eggs filled with a delicate curried mouse). Melon balls marinated in ginger wine.

Harrowgate Champion Shopper

Weird News Stories

> The Hirsel has been renovated and made smaller, and one of the guests at the recent wedding reception of the family's youngest daughter Lady Diana, recalls that the house is 'beautiful, but very simple'.
>
> This, too, is the impression that many people gain from Lady Home herself. 'She is very attractive and charming,' said Mrs V. E. Swinton.
>
> *Yorkshire Post*
>
> Meat Inspector: The successful applicant will be expected to ensure that no food fit for human consumption leaves the slaughterhouse for distribution to the general public.
>
> *Meat Trades Journal*

The incident happened at 2.10 a.m. when the sister was going to the ladies' toilet at the burns unit. The toilet sprang out and slashed her hand with a knife.

St Helens Star

Talented, handsome, well-hung Persian/Burmese stud, preferably vegetarian non-smoker, needed for half Burmese female cat.

Loot (London)

The dead man is described as white, aged between thirty and forty, with an Irish accent.

Bradford Telegraph and Argus

The Complete Cook of Budgerigars $17.95. Birchalls Book Department.

Launceston Examiner

LESOTHO WOMEN MAKE BEAUTIFUL CARPETS
Bangkok World

Detective Chief Inspector James Henderson said he had charged two 61-year-old youths with murder on 24 December and they had been remanded in custody.
Rochdale Observer

HONEYMOON? IF WE CAN FIT IT IN, SAY COUPLE.
Northern Echo

Mr Wedgwood Benn said: 'There is a great revolution under way in education. My education policy is to raise the school leaving age to 65.'
Evening Post

Office Security: Please remember that *all* payments to the Federation should be made by crossed cheques or postal order and not in cash. Help us to make the office less attractive to burglars!
Berkshire Women's Institute newsletter

A large piece of green blotting paper rested on the seat of Prime Minister Harold Wilson today in the House of Commons. It was both symbolic and necessary.
The Times

Thousands of doves and multi-coloured balloons were released as 7800 athletes indulging 1500 women from five continents assembled in the second largest city of the United States.
Pakistan Times

NURSE RAPED By Our Crime Staff
Daily Telegraph

Weird News Stories

Dr James Pike, who died recently in Israel, talks to Oliver Hunkin about psychic phenomena.

The Listener

Atlanta Council's public safety committee voted with some argument – to 'upgrade womanhood' by requiring dancers in nightclubs to wear G-strings and pasties.

News (Adelaide)

Programme change, Southern Television. Sunday 5 July, 4.40 p.m. The Big Film. Delete 'The Prime Minister' and substitute 'The Rat'.

TV Times

'I spent several days in a mental hospital and felt completely at home,' Christopher Mayhew MP, told a meeting of the Sheffield Branch of the Mental Health Association.

Daily Telegraph

A migrant woman thought she had been sent home 'to die' when the hospital told her to go home 'today'. A Migrant Resource Centre spokeswoman said the misunderstanding underlined the need for improved interpreting services in Queensland hospitals.

Herald (Melbourne)

'Hundreds use our service. They know no better.'

Windsor Express

STERILITY MAY BE INHERITED

Pacific Rural News

He pushed what looked like the barrel of a gun into my chest and told me he was going to blow my brains out.

Manchester Evening News

During the war the Queen was presenting awards to a Polish fighter pilot who, during the Battle of Britain, had shot down a record number of Fokkers. She asked him about his most hair-raising exploit.

'I came out of a cloud and found three Fokkers waiting for me. I dived under one of them and shot him down, then another Fokker came up behind me, and I did a left turn and shot him down, then, as the other Fokker dived down on me, I looped the loop and sent him down in flames.'

The Queen nodded admiringly. 'And what were they – Messerschmitts?'

Family & Children's Services Region of Waterloo invites applications to post of: Child Abuse Co-ordinator.

Globe and Mail (Toronto)

The judge said that when the organist started to spend a lot of time at the rectory, Mr James (the vicar) warned his wife 'not to get into a position from which it might be difficult to withdraw'.

Evening Standard

Wedding gown worn once by mistake. Size 9–10. Asking $20.

Oshawa Times

ONE LEGGED ESCAPEE RAPIST STILL ON THE RUN

Weekend Australian

The Cats Protection League is holding a flea market in Bardwell Court, Dereham, on Saturday 2 March from 9.30 a.m.

Norfolk Advertiser

Weird News Stories

FIRE MAY HAVE CAUSED BLAZE

Barnet Borough Times

Marketing Executive: Post-secondary education – Kowledge in marketing research – Good command in written Engliqh ald Ahilese – Illitiatite and creative.

South China Morning Post

Question: I have an Irish terrier bitch, which ignores the doorbell. How can I train her to be a watch?
Answer (the vet): Each time the doorbell rings, jump up excitedly and bark yourself.

Evening Telegraph

The artificial insemination of animals is taken for granted to improve the breed and product. Human insemination is a different ball-game.

Catholic Register (Canada)

Pensions for Clergy. Removal of evil principle from parish life.

Yorkshire Post

People who travel on trains without a reasonable excuse will be summonsed and may face fines of up to $200.

Newcastle Herald

English Spanish shorthand Typist. Efficien. Useless. Apply Otherwise.

Advertisement in Spanish newspaper

Three Polish fighter pilots were attending a party given by an English hostess during World War II. The hostess asked one of them if he had children. 'No. My wife is inconceivable.'

The second pilot intervened to explain: 'No, he means his wife is unbearable.'

The third pilot shook his head. 'You must pardon their English. What they mean to say is that his wife is impregnable.'

In its In-flight Film Guide for September 1993, Continental Airlines listed Kenneth Branagh's *Much Ado About Nothing* under the heading: 'Branagh and the Bard'. On the opposite page, the French translation reads: 'Branagh et the Lard'. In fact, lard is not French for bard, but for bacon. One literate passenger was heard to remark that the compiler of the Guide was obviously a Baconian – one of those who believe

---

On a recent visit to the Ongar public lending library this notice was observed in the *Eastern Gazette*:

The authorities at Ongar library have received a number of complaints about a card in the index file with an entry which read: SEX: SEE LIBRARIAN. This has now been changed. The new entry reads: SEX: FOR SEX ASK AT THE DESK.

A visit to the local Ongar junior school, however, yielded the following misunderstandings of the Lord's Prayer: 'Give us this day our day in bed' and 'Lead us not into Thames Station'. One child had understood that the wafers given during communion were 'Cheesus Christ'. Another was gaily chirping along to the sign of the cross 'in the name of the Father and of the Son and into the 'ole he goes'.

In the Nuts (unground) (other than ground nuts)
Order, the expression nuts shall have reference to
such nuts, other than ground nuts, as would but for
this amending Order not qualify as nuts (unground)
(other than ground nuts) by reason of their being
nuts (underground).
Amendment to British Parliamentary Act

that William Shakespeare was really Francis Bacon – and
that this was his covert method of introducing his belief
about the true authorship of *Much Ado About Nothing* into
the Film Guide.

The court was told that soon after the party came into
Maloney's Bar, Milligan spat at O'Flaherty and called him a
'stinking Ulsterman'. O'Flaherty punched Milligan, and
Rourke hit him with a bottle. Milligan kicked O'Flaherty in
the groin and threw a pint of beer in Rourke's face. This led
to ill-feeling, and they began to fight.

County Louth (Eire) newspaper

East German swimmer Sylvia Ester set a world 100-metres
record of 57.9 seconds in 1967 – but officials refused to
recognize it because she swam in the nude.

West Briton

Danish police are trying to trace women who own 577
panties, bras and stockings of all shapes and sizes stolen
from clotheslines at Holstebro in western Denmark. A
thirty-four-year-old man has been charged with theft.

Western Morning News

Counterfeit fifty-dollar Federal Reserve notes seized in

Milan, Italy, bore the words, 'redeemable in awful currency of the United States Treasury'.

New York Times

An overstressed traffic policeman in Bangkok Thailand was taken to mental hospital after switching all the lights green and dancing amid the ensuing chaos. The twenty-five-year-old officer, stationed at one of the city's worst crossroads, nicknamed Hell Intersection, was diagnosed as suffering from severe stress.

Western Morning News

Quote: 'Quoting the Queen, Sir Norman admitted that last year had been an "anus horribilis".'

Daily Telegraph

A tenant found a unique way to keep his council house as warm as toast – insulating the loft with Edam cheese. Workmen calling to insulate the home in Loughton, Essex, were amazed to find the work already done with several thousand pieces of the Dutch cheese's distinctive red coating.

Western Morning News

Indiana's Governor Matthew E. Welsh informed an audience that, despite problems, strides are being made in certain areas, including education. He was informed by the Department of Correction of a reformatory prisoner who, while serving a term for armed robbery, was taught to read and write in the institution's education program. 'Now he's serving a term for forgery,' concluded the governor. 'And I say this is progress.'

Roger Allen

Weird News Stories

When two convicts who escaped from a Texas prison were caught in a couple of days through a phone call from a farmer a hundred miles distant, newsmen converged on the farmer. 'How could you recognize them when you've never seen a picture of them?' they asked.

'When those two fellas walked by I was out plowin',' he replied. 'Of course I waved and hollered, but they just walked on. So I knew they wasn't local folks, and then I remembered about the convicts. I figured they was the only kind of folks that'd be in too big a hurry to stop for a chat.'

Jean Mikeska

Mr Michael Vanner, of Bexhill Road, St Leonards, a defendant in a recent case at Hastings Magistrates' Court, wishes to state that Mr Melvin Peck whom he pleaded not guilty to assaulting, was not a passer-by, as stated, but a friend of his.

Sussex newspaper

Rats and cockroaches raiding the stores – not unscrupulous policemen with an eye for resale value – accounted for the loss of £17,000 worth of illegal drugs seized from addicts in the Philippines, a police chief said.

Western Evening News

A glossy American cookbook contained a recipe for Silky Caramel Slices: put an unopened can of condensed milk in a pot and leave it on the stove for four hours. The publishers later recalled all the books at vast expense, when they realized they had just invented the first exploding pudding – they had forgotten to mention that the pot should first be filled with water.

Reader's Digest

With more than sixty sashes of honour in Prince Philip's dressing room, it was perhaps an accident waiting to happen.

But few could have expected the embarrassment of his attendance at the funeral of King Baudouin of Belgium last month.

Instead of the deep purple of Belgium's Grand Cordon of the Order of Leopold, he wore the green, red and gold of Zaire's Order of the Leopard. To make matters worse, although Zaire was once a Belgian colony the two countries no longer have any links.

Baudouin is even said to have ordered that President Mobutu of Zaire should be barred from the funeral.

Onlookers at the service, attended by royalty and heads of state from all over the world, were astonished at the blunder.

And the Prince is said to be furious with the member of his household responsible for the mix-up.

Buckingham Palace claimed yesterdey that the sash was that of the military division of the Order of Leopold from the former Belgian Congo. But there is no mention of any such honour in a detailed record in Debrett's of sixty-three decorations awarded to him.

Western Morning News

'Intersection Six is still being planned,' said a spokesman for the Department of the Environment. Asked where it was going to be, the spokesman replied: 'We aren't quite sure but I imagine it would be between Intersection Five and Intersection Seven.'

Manchester Evening News

All meat in this window is from local farmers killed on the premises.

Sign in a Somerset butcher's shop

The FBI agent in a Western state was hot on the trail of a fugitive. When word came that he was heading for a small town, the G-man called the local sheriff. 'You send me a pitcher of that guy and I'll git him good,' the sheriff promised. That night the agent mailed the sheriff a dozen pictures of the wanted man – profiles, fullface, standing, sitting and in various costumes. Shortly he received an electrifing telephone call: 'We got eleven of those crooks locked up already,' the sheriff boasted. 'And I guarantee to jug the last one before morning!'

Fulton Oursler

A restaurant that gave a new meaning to after-dinner sweets has been ordered by health officials to use plates – and not the bellies of its topless waitresses – to serve dessert. The restaurant in Perth, Australia, invited diners to eat fruit salad and cream off the stomach of a waitress.

Western Morning News

A Minneapolis suburb has been buzzing with the news that a housewife was seen holding hands with the mailman on her front porch. True, the lady in question calmly admits. It was the best way she could think of to convince her dog that postmen aren't burglars.

'Almanac' in *Minneapolis Tribune*

A very disagreeable mistake was made by the police-constables stationed at St Austell, a few days ago. A lunatic, an Irishman, had escaped from the county asylum at Bodmin, and the St Austell police seeing an Irishman in the town, and evidently thinking that all natives of the Green Isle are rather cracky, and that this one would do quite as well as the other, marched him off to the lock-up, followed by a lot of boys, although the man had resided in the higher quarter of the town for years. The unlucky prisoner told his captors to go with him to the rate-collector, who would satisfy them that he was not a lunatic, as he had just been paying him a lot of rates, but without effect. After arriving at the police-station, however, he was soon liberated.

West Briton

Western Morning News was wrongly illustrated with a picture of another hallucinogenic fungus, the fly agaric, which is extremely poisonous if eaten and can prove fatal. We apologise for the error.

Western Morning News

Two colleagues, waiting in a Catholic church while Klemperer went to confession, were surprised when, after rather a long time, he emerged from the confessional, slamming the door and shouting, 'that's enough!'

Klemperer Stories

Pope escapes.

Guardian

Advice from Granny:

Lily Savage, drag queen: My granny, Erica von Savage, was a compulsive liar: she told us she was an international spy but in reality she worked as a chambermaid on the Isle of Man. The only piece of advice I took off her was: 'God will protect us, but to make sure carry a brick in your handbag.'

Marje Proops, agony aunt: My granny taught me to play poker when I was eight. She was a wicked old bird but she looked like an angel. She gave out sound wisdom about gentlemen poker-players too. My own grandchildren tell me all about their sex problems. I never give advice, though.

Andrew Logan, sculptor: I remember my granny sitting in a crochet shawl glued to the boxing on the television. The only advice she gave me was to sit up straight and behave.

Christina Dodwell, explorer: My granny used to tell me: 'If you don't try it, you'll never know if you like it.' Her words came back to me when I was sharing bowls of maggots with the local people in New Guinea.

Lizzie Spivey, film production manager: My husband wanted me to move from the Cotswolds – where I was surrounded by family and friends – to Cheshire. My grandmother said: 'You don't want to be going up there, do you?' I realized I didn't, and now I'm happily divorced.

Sunday Independent

Chapter Six

Hollywood Tales
and Quotes

Victor Young went to enormous lengths to play a practical joke on fellow film-composer Max Steiner. Young happened to be in the studio when the orchestra was trying out the love theme of *Now Voyager* ('Would It Be Wrong To Kiss'), and jotted it down.

A few evenings later, Steiner came to Young's house to play cards. At eleven p.m., someone suggested turning on the radio to get the local news. After the announcer had introduced the programme, there came a blast of music – Steiner's love theme. Steiner leapt to his feet with a howl of anguish. 'That's my theme – they've stolen my music.'

'That's impossible,' said Young, 'that programme has been on for years and they've always used that theme to introduce it.' 'I tell you it's my theme,' howled Steiner, now almost hysterical.

At that point Young admitted what he'd done: how he had orchestrated the theme and had it recorded by the orchestra for whom he was then writing a score, and finally how he had cut the recording into a tape of the local news programme, recorded the previous day.

Max Wilk

Bette Davis on a starlet: 'There goes the good time that was had by all.'

Actress Tallulah Bankhead: 'I'm as pure as the driven slush.'

127

Weird News Stories

Hollywood writers Ben Hecht and Charles MacArthur formed a Hollywood chamber music group which included Harpo Marx and composer George Antheil. Groucho Marx, who played mandolin, was excluded. On the evening the group met to rehearse in an upper room of Ben Hecht's house, Groucho interrupted the session by flinging open the door and shouting, 'Quiet, please.' When he was gone, the group speculated what he was up to, the general view being that he was jealous. Soon after, the door opened again, and Groucho shouted: 'Quiet, you lousy amateurs.' He disappeared downstairs, and minutes later the house was shaken by the sound of the *Tannhäuser* overture played at full volume. They rushed downstairs to find that the complete Los Angeles Symphony Orchestra – about a hundred men – had been squeezed into Hecht's sitting room, and that Groucho was conducting them with sweeping gestures. He had sneaked them into the house one by one during the evening.

The chamber music group decided it would be less trouble to admit Groucho and his mandolin.

Max Wilk

Dorothy Parker: 'If all the girls attending the Yale Prom were laid end to end, I wouldn't be at all surprised.'

Dorothy Parker, when told that socialite Claire Booth Luce was always kind to her inferiors, asked: 'Wherever does she find them?'

Groucho Marx: I've been around so long I knew Doris Day before she was a virgin.'

Groucho Marx to his hostess as he left a party: 'I've had a lovely evening. But this wasn't it.'

Groucho Marx: 'A man is only as old as the woman he feels.'

Groucho Marx: 'Anyone who says he can see through women is missing a lot.'

W. C. Fields: 'If at first you don't succeed, try, try again. Then give up. No use being a damn fool about it.'

Film star Ava Gardner: 'Deep down I'm pretty superficial.'

Woody Allen: 'If my film makes even one more person miserable, I feel I've done my job.'

Woody Allen: 'It's not that I'm afraid to die. I just don't want to be there when it happens.'

Joe Frisco on Hollywood smog: 'This is the only town where you can wake up and hear the birds coughing in the trees.'

Novelist and screen writer Scott Fitzgerald: 'You always knew where you stood with Sam Goldwyn – nowhere . . .'

Sid Grauman said: 'I saw this empty taxicab drive up, and out stepped Sam Goldwyn.'

Goldwyn instructed his lawyer to make enquiries about buying the novel *The Well of Loneliness*. 'But boss,' said the

Sam Goldwyn: 'Anyone who goes to a psychiatrist should
have his head examined'

Peter Sellers once went to a party in the country at which he danced all night with a very beautiful stranger. He was quite captivated by her charming looks and personality and determined to accompany her home. They left the party together and Peter thought his luck was in. There was a full moon and the evening was warm. Perhaps, suggested Mr Sellers tentatively, he might be allowed to accompany his lovely companion along the bridle path?

'Oh no, I'm terribly sorry,' was her immediate and frank response, 'it's far too early to be thinking about marriage.'

---

lawyer, 'you can't make that – it's about lesbians.' Goldwyn growled: 'Make 'em Austrians.'

Sam Goldwyn, recommending his latest picture to a friend: 'You ought to see my *Hans Christian Andersen*. It's full of charmth and warmth.'

'I tell you, Marion,' said Goldwyn to comedienne Marion Davies, 'you don't know what life is all about until you've found yourself lying on the brink of a great abscess.'

Goldwyn, refusing to listen to Eddie Cantor's pleas about cutting a scene: 'It's no use, Eddie, you've got to take the bull by the teeth.'

After the preview of *All Quiet on the Western Front*, a nervous executive asked: 'Isn't there any way we could give it a happy ending?'

The actual line in the Warner Bros World War II film *Casablanca* is not 'Play it Again, Sam' at all. It is not even Humphrey Bogart who utters the words. In fact it is Ingrid Bergman who says to the piano-playing Dooley Wilson, 'Play it, Sam. Play "As Time Goes By".'

In any event, Sam doesn't play, he merely sings, since Dooley Wilson couldn't actually play the piano, the sound of which was dubbed in at a later date.

Max Wilk

Goldwyn explained the crowds at Louis B. Mayer's funeral: 'The only reason so many people showed up was to make sure he was dead.'

Film producer Harry Cohn: 'Give me two years and I'll make her an overnight star.'

Harry Cohn, after sacking a director: 'Never let that bastard back in here – unless we need him.'

Comedian Red Skelton, on the crowds at Harry Cohn's funeral: 'It proves what they always say: give the public what they want and they'll come out for it.'

When Ray Bradbury was working with John Huston on the film script of *Moby Dick*, Huston came in one day waving a telegram signed 'Jack Warner' which declared: 'CANNOT PROCEED WITH FILM UNLESS SEXY FEMALE ROLE ADDED.' Bradbury almost became hysterical. 'Has the man gone insane? We can't have a woman on the ship . . .' 'That's

Robert Benchley's doctor was an indefatigable
inventor of new cures, and the obliging Benchley
allowed himself to be used as a guinea pig. One day
the doctor asked his cooperation to try out a pill
for restoring sexual potency.

The day after he had taken the pill, the doctor
called to ask if he had noticed any change, and put
him through a catechism: temperature, sexual
excitement, etc. To each question Benchley replied
in the negative.

'There must have been *some* change,' said the
disappointed doctor.

'Only this,' said Benchley, dropping his pyjamas,
and revealing a sprouting of cock tail-feathers at
the base of his spine.

Benchley had glued them on with the help of his
actor friend Roland Young.

Max Wilk

Hollywood, Ray,' said Huston, shaking his head. 'Maybe
Ahab could have an affair with Gina Lollobrigida as a
disguised stowaway.'

Just as Bradbury looked like having apoplexy, Huston
flung himself on the couch, doubled up with laughter, and
Bradbury realized it was a practical joke.

Max Wilk

Orson Welles on pop singer Donny Osmond: 'He has Van
Gogh's ear for music.'

Hollywood writer Gene Fowler on an editor: 'He should have
a pimp for a brother so he'd have somebody to look up to.'

Charles MacArthur regarded himself as a formidable chess player. One day some friends told him they had met a Spaniard called José Raùl, who wanted a match. MacArthur agreed immediately.

An unusually large number of friends appeared to watch the match. It was not until he was some way into the game that MacArthur guessed – from his opponent's formidable skill – that he was actually the world chess champion Capablanca.

Max Wilk

'Well,' said the director, 'we could have the Germans win the war.'

Hollywood writer Wilson Mizner on Jack Warner: 'He has oilcloth pockets so he can steal soup.'

Columnist Walter Winchell on Hollywood: 'The place where they shoot too many pictures and not enough actors.'

Herman Manciewicz on Louis B. Mayer: 'There but for the grace of God goes God.'

Arthur Sheekman, a Hollywood writer, tells of a fellow writer who, late one afternoon, received a note signed 'Jack Warner'. It explained that he was considering making a film of *War and Peace,* and asked the writer to read it overnight and make a quick assessment.

The writer learned that it was a practical joke only when he went into Warner's office – after a sleepless night – and asked if Warner needed a story outline.

Comedian Will Rogers on Congress: 'Every time they make a joke it's a law, and every time they make a law, it's a joke.'

Robert Benchley was part of a school of card players in the Algonquin Hotel. Asked if he didn't mind that another player went to the lavatory so often, he replied: 'No, it's the only time I know what he's got in his hand.'

Robert Benchley: 'It took me fifteen years to discover I had no talent for writing, but by that time I couldn't give it up – I was too famous.'

Much-married film star Mickey Rooney: 'I'm the only man who has a marriage licence made out To Whom It May Concern.'

Actor Beerbohm Tree, to a man in the street who was staggering under the weight of a grandfather clock: 'My poor fellow, why not carry a watch?'

Chapter Seven

It Cannot Be True

In 1958 the West Midlands Police Force thought that they had come up with the ultimate solution for traffic control – a helmet with a flashing blue lamp on top.

The helmet, fitted with a battery-powered light, was top heavy and kept falling off every time PC Jim Sparks – the lucky constable selected for the test run – tried to turn his head to watch the oncoming cars.

'A right Charlie I felt, too,' he said. 'People were staring at me open-mouthed as they drove past. I'd never been so embarrassed. It was before fluorescent clothing and it could be downright dangerous on traffic duty – you had to be pretty nimble on your feet – but the flashing helmet wasn't any use. The chin strap dug into me and, because it was so heavy with the batteries in the top of the helmet, it was just about impossible to control. Every time I moved my head, the helmet simply fell off.'

After PC Sparks had fought valiantly with the helmet for over an hour and a half, senior officers conceded that the idea might be a mistake. The prototype headgear disappeared into the mists of time until Mr Sparks, now retired, responded to a call from West Midlands Police Museum in Birmingham for memorabilia. 'When they saw the photograph,' he said, 'they couldn't believe it and they all fell about laughing.'

This is a picture of a policeman with a light on his head

Lunatic General

The appointment of Sir William Erskine as a senior commander during the Peninsular War was a mistake to rival the very best. The Duke of Wellington was astonished at the commission and wrote immediately to the Military Secretary in London to complain that Erskine was well-known to be barking mad. 'No doubt he is a little mad at times,' replied the Secretary by post, 'but in his lucid intervals he is a jolly nice chap . . . though I must say that he did look a little mad as he embarked.' Erskine's record wasn't too impressive either. His astonishingly bad eyesight had made him a complete liability at the battle of Sabugal in 1811, where he had led a charge *away from the enemy* by mistake.

At the battle of Almeida, all of Wellington's forebodings were fulfilled. The Iron Duke was closing in on the besieged

It was a hot day in Henley. A fire broke out in the locality and the occupants of the worst hit house telephoned the local fire brigade who were all 'Indisposed' since they were taking part in a simulated fire drill on an imaginary inferno miles away.

Distressed, the occupants called the next nearest fire station, which wasn't near at all. Some time later an engine came crawling up the local hill which was all too much for its ancient parts. The cab burst into flames and the firemen clambered out, spewing up all over the pavement. It was then impossible to use the suction pump since it was all clogged up with smoke.

Quite by chance, the local fire engine just then happened to come tootling past and stopped to see what was going on. They were, however, unable actually to assist since they had no water left on board having just used it all up and in the process waterlogging the village green on which they had just been practising their dummy run.

Whilst the first and second fire crews stopped passing motorists and asked them to help put out the fire in the engine, all the locals got together and put out the fire in the house using that well-known fire-fighting device, running up and down with buckets.

French garrison and victory seemed assured. Aware of the dangers of placing too much on the madman's shoulders, Wellington asked him to perform the simple task of guarding the bridge of Barba de Puerca. There were no charges to be made and no pitfalls into which Erskine's loopiness or his short-sightedness could lead him. He just had to stand there with a mixed battalion of cavalry and infantry and stop the French getting out.

Erskine was having dinner when Wellington's order arrived. His first response (madder than even Wellington could have anticipated) was to send a corporal and four men to guard the bridge. One of the other dinner guests was so shocked by this stupidity that he blurted out, 'Sir William, you might as well attempt to block up the bridge with a pinch of snuff.'

This brought on one of Erskine's famous moments of lucidity. He immediately wrote out an order to send a whole regiment to block the bridge. 'Better safe than sorry,' he added.

Unfortunately, this moment of lucidity was a particularly brief one. As soon as he had finished writing out the order, Erskine folded it up, put it in his pocket and forgot about it. When the French realized the danger of their position and decided to retreat, they were amazed to find the bridge unguarded and escaped without a single casualty. Wellington called it 'the most disgraceful military event that has yet occurred to us'.

When Erskine subsequently committed suicide by jumping out of a window in Lisbon in 1813, his last words were: 'Why on earth did I do that?'

Plain Cuckoo

'One of Colorado's oldest citizens and a resident of Walsenburg for about a century died here yesterday. Mrs Quintina was 104 years old at the time of her death, her grandmother said.'

Enterprise Times, Brockton, Massachusetts

Ronald the Toast-Maker

In 1952 Ronald Reagan was in Brazil at a political function and, towards the end of the meal, he was asked to make a speech.

'Now would you join me in a toast to President Figueiredo,' he said, 'and to all the people of Bolivia . . . oh no, that's wrong, that's where I'm going next . . . erm . . . to the people of Brazil, yes that's right, Brazil.' His voice trailed off as one of his aides drew his attention to the fact that his next destination was in fact Bogota, the capital of Colombia.

Mad Jimmy Carter

'A great man who should have been President and would have been one of the greatest Presidents in history – Hubert Horatio Hornblower.' Jimmy Carter at the 1950 Democratic Convention on Hubert Humphrey.

Cereal Killer

Pat Coombs, a comedienne of the 1970s, holds the record for the highest number of mistakes in one shoot on a television commercial. In 1973 she astonished her camera crew by forgetting the name of the product she was supposed to be advertising on a record-breaking twenty-eight takes. This truly stupendous feat of memory is still with her since, on being questioned about the advertisement five years after the event, she was still unable to remember anything beyond the fact that it was a kind of Swiss breakfast cereal.

Shortly afterwards the product was withdrawn. Ms Coombs no longer eats muesli.

In November 1983 a nightclub boss and local gang leader, Jimmy 'the Beard' Ferrozo, was engaged in a sex romp at one of his clubs, the Condor, with a twenty-three-year-old stripper called Teresa Hill.

As they writhed around on the top of the club's baby grand piano, after closing hours, Teresa's spine came into contcct with the button that caused the piano to rise up slowly from the floor. Jimmy and Teresa were otherwise occupied and didn't notice their sudden rise in status. The romp ended quite suddenly as the piano reached the ceiling. Miss Hill screamed for help and firemen arrived to rescue the unfulfilled couple. Teresa was pulled out, naked and bruised. But Jimmy was already dead.

Fighting for Survival

In May 1981 two old men, who had been living opposite each other in Cleveland, Ohio for fifty years, had finally had enough.

The men, one aged seventy-seven and one aged seventy-six, began quarrelling in their mutual hallway at about 11 a.m. on Tuesday. Neither would give way and so they both went back into their apartments and came out with antique pistols. They were standing just five feet apart during the duel and fired six shots each. All twelve bullets went astray. Police theorized that they missed because one needed a cane to prop himself up whilst firing, and the other had trouble with his vision since he suffered from acute glaucoma.

Residents called the police, who took the pair to the local

station for interview. 'There were bullet holes above, bullet holes below and bullet holes all over the hallway,' said one of the detectives, 'but none anywhere about the person of either of the old folk.'

The men were released after both signed papers saying that they did not wish to press charges against the other. Police kept the guns which may go into the local museum.

Kinky Devils

During the seventies the telekinetic powers of Uri Geller, who was best known for his ability to bend metal objects by merely looking at them, were much in vogue. So much so that a young lady in Sweden took out court proceedings against him for causing her unwanted pregnancy. She claimed that as a result of the fact that she and her boyfriend had been watching him on the television whilst making love on the sofa her IUD had been warped and rendered useless.

Pill Talk

The politician, Sir Alan Sterling Parks, declared in 1970 that 'no woman should be kept on the pill for 20 years until, in fact, a sufficient number have been kept on the pill for 20 years'.

Loch Ness Monster

The dominating geographical feature of the Scottish Highlands is, of course, the Great Glen, a rift valley sixty miles long which splits the country in two and contains, on its bed, three of Scotland's most famous Lochs – Lochy, Oich and Ness. Of these Loch Ness is undoubtedly the most famous and the most spectacular. Eight rivers feed into it and it is deeper than the North Sea and most of the Atlantic Ocean. It has never been known to freeze. It is very, very long and very, very narrow and its steep wooded banks form a wind-funnel giving rise, at times, to immensely beautiful but tidal-like waves.

It is most likely these physical properties that gave rise to the legend of the Loch Ness Monster – or Nessiteras Rhombopteryx, as Sir Peter Scott dubbed the doughty dino in the mad mid-eighties. The dotty knight was responsible for a huge amount of serious interest in the 'old lady of the lake' until a clever TV pundit noticed that Nessiteras Rhombopteryx was an anagran of 'Monster Hoax By Sir Peter S'.

Mistaken sightings of Nessie are legion. The first known report was in the sixth century. St Adamnan, who was a very spiritual man and not known for a propensity to tell lies, reports, in his biography of St Columba, that he saw her as he sailed up the Loch on his way to convert the town of Inverness. Nessie, he said, began to cause rough surfaces and the sailing boat rocked violently as the sailors' stomachs churned and their faces turned green with both fear and nausea. St Columba stood up in the boat and as Nessie's head rose from the surface to face one of the monks in a head-on confrontation Columba spoke soothing words and calmed the fearsome beast who sank slowly and calmly back into the icy depths.

A sixteenth-century chronicle describes 'a terrible beast issuing out of the water early one morning about midsummer, knocking down trees and killing three men with its tail'. But sightings were sporadic until the twentieth century when they began to proliferate like crazy, which perhaps has something to do with Nessie's profound effect on local business. An organist from Westminster Cathedral swore he saw her in 1973; and in 1961 as many as thirty guests at a local hotel saw two humps appear in a sudden explosion of surf and swim along the surface of the Loch for fifteen minutes before sinking. A circus owner called Bertram Mills offered a £20,000 reward to anyone who could capture the monster for his circus but no one ever did. Possibly the least successful attempt to do so was that of four firemen from Hemel Hempstead in 1975 who decided that where all of the other hunters had gone wrong was on the gender of Nessie, who must, being a monster, naturally be a man.

They built a thirty-foot long papier mâché lady monster to attract their Mr Ness and completed it with false eyelashes, full make-up and a pre-recorded mating call. Possibly their first mistake was that the pre-recorded sound turned out to be that of a male walrus and thus unlikely to attract a conservative monster from the deep; secondly, their outboard motor developed a fault, the boat went into a spin and the paper monster's behind was instantaneously flattened by an unfortunately placed jetty, which could hardly have made her the irresistible object they had hoped for.

Loony Bike

In 1897 Thomas Bennet of 69 High Holborn announced a splendid new design of bicycle.

The front wheel and handlebars looked pretty much the same as they do on a modern bike. The pedals, however, were mounted on a single huge cog communicating directly with a tiny cog at the centre of the back wheel.

The back wheel was very unusual. It was heavy and spoked and had sixteen free-spinning tiny wheels mounted around the edge. The crucial element to Adam's design was that the driver should sit directly on top of this curious wheel. As the pedals went round forwards, the central back wheel would rotate backwards and the tiny wheels around the edge would sort of squidge the cycle forwards. As Adams explained it:

'The weight of the rider is perpendicular to the centre of the small wheel which is under him. Immediately the toothed wheel is turned ever so little by the larger toothed wheel from the crank, the weight of the rider is lifted off the centre of the small wheel under him. This, coupled with the power put forth by the rider on to the pedal, causes the smaller wheel under him to, as it were, slip from under him with tremendous velocity (the heavier the rider the greater the velocity) on to the next small wheel.'

The principle of the thing, thought Adams, was the same as that by which a roller-skater fell over: 'when the hind wheels of the skate slip forward from under him, his weight goes off the centre and he loses his equilibrium and goes on to the back of his head with great force (the heavier the man, the heavier he falls).'

'If the skater could have only kept his equilibrium,' explains Adams, 'he would have gone forward as fast as his skate travelled, instead of being left behind on the floor.' By this process, the mad inventor thought that his bicycle could travel at sixty miles per hour.

The number of mistakes involved in this design is frighteningly high. Adams ignores every law of motion in constructing his potty bike. As the modern scientist Alan Sutton points out in his book *A Victorian World of Science* (Iowa, 1986), any rider pedalling Adams's bike would remain stock still. The ludicrous back wheel would simply whizz round, with all the little wheels spinning in the opposite direction as they hit the ground or the rider's bottom, which would be horribly bruised by the whole

performance.
Green Fingers, No Eyes

Thomas Nuttall (1786–1859) was a scientist with spectacularly little sense of direction. He was, by training, a botanist and went travelling on unsuccessful expeditions all over north-west America. During one trip in 1812, his fellow scientists had to light beacons every evening in order to guide him back to their encampment.

On one sad occasion when he got completely lost, a search party was sent out to retrieve him. Nuttall saw the team coming towards him through the darkness and, rather neurotically, assumed that they were Indians out to capture him. He therefore fled and was finally tracked down three days later when he, quite by accident, wandered straight back into the camp. His most pathetic mistake, however, must be the occasion on which he got so lost that he simply collapsed and went to sleep. A passing Indian came across him and, instead of scalping him, considered him so utterly useless that he carried him three miles up the river and took him back to the camp.

Chapter Eight

Foot in Mouth

Sam Goldwyn, the film mogul, was very well-known for his verbal mistakes. On one occasion he was considering making a film about Jesus and the Last Supper. He felt it needed a bit of extra something and that the cast just wasn't quite spectacular enough. 'Why only twelve disciples?' he enquired. 'Go out and get thousands.'

He was also heard to say that 'a verbal contract isn't worth the paper it's written on' and on one memorable afternoon, he commissioned an up-and-coming sculptor to create a piece for him with the words 'I want you to make a bust of my wife's hands'. On another occasion a number of the crew on a particular film set had all been involved in a rather trying dispute. In attempting to placate as many of the argumentative technical staff as possible, Goldwyn stood up to make a pacifying speech which began, 'We have all passed a lot of water since last week.'

Other verbal mistakes for which he was famed included:

'Why did you name your baby Arthur? Every Tom, Dick and Harry is called Arthur.'

'Let's have some new clichés.'

'A bachelor's life is no life for a single man' and, my particular favourite:

'Anybody who goes to see a psychiatrist ought to have his head examined.'

In 1954 Winston Churchill paid a visit to the engineering plant at Harwell and on arrival, was taken on an extensive

On a flight across the United States a potential
hijacker suddenly pulled out a revolver on one of
the air stewardesses as she went past him.

'Take me to Detroit,' he bellowed.

'That happens to be our appointed destination,
Sir,' she replied politely.

'Oh, OK then,' said the gunman, who put his
revolver back into his pocket and sat down
again.

tour of the machine works. He stopped from time to time as
he walked around and chatted to the scientists, asking them
politely about their work. The first scientist replied, 'I make
heavy water into uranium,' and Churchill nodded politely.
He went up to a second scientist and asked him, in turn,
what it was that he did. 'I make light water to make
uranium,' replied the technician. Churchill thought about
this for a moment and then replied, 'I want to make
ordinary water but I can't find the urinium.'

Mrs Margaret Friend, aged forty-eight, of Southend on Sea
was arrested and brought to the local magistrates court on
a charge of prostitution. She was outraged and, in a spirit of
judicial enquiry, the court asked her to assist them by

On 13 February 1979 Britain's leading architects
met at Skegness Pier to hand over an award for
best designed pier theatre to a very talented fellow
called George Sunderland.

During the presentation ceremony a storm
broke and the theatre was swept out to sea.

explaining why it was, exactly, that the charge could not possibly be correct.

'Oh,' she exclaimed, 'there's no way I could ever be a prostitute. I'm far too short-sighted. I'm blind in one eye and only have partial vision in the other. In fact, I can only ever see anyone if they're right on top of me.'

On the occasion of General de Gaulle's retirement, the French leader decided to celebrate by inviting a large number of political dignitaries and their spouses to lunch. Amongst the many illustrious world leaders present at the table were Dorothy and Harold Macmillan.

Dorothy talked at great length about the remarkable contribution that de Gaulle had made to French history and then, turning to his wife, asked Mrs de Gaulle what she was most looking forward to, now that she had a little more time on her hands.

Mrs de Gaulle beamed away at Mrs Macmillan and, with everyone at the table silent and expectant, she opened her mouth to reply with the words:

'What I most look forward to now is a penis.'

There was a stunned silence around the table, whilst some of the primmer guests shuffled around on their seats, blushing and embarrassed. General de Gaulle himself rapidly intervened, explaining carefully to his wife that the word was not pronounced in quite that way. She had not been looking forward to 'a penis' but, in fact, to 'happiness'.

'I have just learned that we do have the film of the astronauts' breakfast, which should be coming up shortly.'
(Frank McGee – BBC News)

'Former Wimbledon champion Martina Navratilova had a surprisingly easy victory over Andrea Jaegar in the final of the Avon Tournament in Seattle today. She won in straight sex.'

(BBC News)

'Well the streakers are at it again, this time at a local football game just outside of Boston. I can't figure out this type of behaviour – I guess they just want to show us they're nuts.'
(Larry Glick of WBZ News, Boston, Massachusetts)

Lord Portarlingon was invited to an important political occasion at which he walked straight into Queen Victoria. Jumping backwards, in a rather surprised way, the lord recovered himself and looking up at her was heard to say, 'Damn it, Ma'am, I know your face but I cannot put a name to it.'

Funny-faced comedian Stephen Fry came up with some splendid royal bricks on the TV show *Whose Line is it Anyway?* Fry was asked to think of things that you shouldn't say when you meet the Queen. His first response was the amazing line 'Whop some skull on that, bitch' – delivered almost too fast for the audience to hear. After delivering the fateful words, Fry was plunged into embarrassment and apology and came up with a surreal follow-up gag. 'Oh that reminds me,' said Fry to the imaginary monarch, 'I must buy a stamp.'

'This is a great day for France.'
(Richard Nixon in 1974 at the funeral of President Georges Pompidou)

In December 1975 President Gerald Ford drank the health of Anwar Sadat, the leader of Egypt, toasting loudly to 'the President of Israel'.

'I just wanna say,' said Mayor Richard Daley of Chicago at a fun-pedal convention for married couple cyclists, 'you husbands and wives, if you wanna get along together, you gotta get one of them tantrum bicycles.'

Laura Corrigan, a famous jet-setter of international repute, amazed her friends by her splendid malapropism after having been to the doctor for indigestive problems. 'My doctor told me,' she said, 'if you want to avoid indigestion, you must masturbate, masturbate, masturbate.'

A current member of parliament tells this story of his early love life, which he, presumably, now regrets:

'When I was an undergraduate, I developed a consuming passion for a very pretty Welsh woman called Myfanwy Lewis. Myfanwy had a lot of admirers and the only way I could get close to her was by swearing blind that I had no sexual interest in her at all, which I did at every opportunity. Eventually, we became friends and I began to ponder what my next move should be.

'Towards the summer, when love was in the air, and we knew each other quite well, I invited Myfanwy around for dinner with two friends of mine called David and Harriet who were very much a couple. The evening passed off pretty well and after the meal we were all a bit tipsy and having a good deal of fun. Then, as spirits rose, David and Myfanwy suddenly got into a terrible drunken row which became more and more heated. Within seconds, David had screamed abuse and left, taking Harriet with him and leaving Myfanwy on my sofa in floods of tears. I went over and hugged her as she clung to me for dear life and bawled her eyes out.

'This was almost more than I could bear and it was everything I could do to offer the reassurances that were required without exploding. After fifteen minutes or so, in which I considered I was putting on a pretty good show, Myfanwy suddenly pulled out the rug from under my feet by shouting "It's no good. It's no good. You're pretending to be nice. But all you really want to do is to sleep with me."

'I thought about this one pretty hard and planned my response carefully. "Myfanwy, Myfanwy," I exclaimed resolutely, revelling in the mere sound of her magical name, "the thought of kissing you had not even entered my mind." But it didn't come out like that. Instead, the fateful words were uttered: "Myfanwy, Myfanwy. The thought of kissing you had not even entered my mouth."

What's in a Name

About halfway through his period of office as the British Ambassador to Cairo, Sir Miles Lampton was knighted in the New Year's Honours List and, overnight, became Lord Killearn. A little while later he and his wife threw a party to celebrate this auspicious event and invited some of the important people who lived in the country. One of these came up to the new Lord Killearn and, grasping his hand and greeting him warmly, he introduceel himself and pointed out that he was so glad to meet the couple at last. It was so pleasant to have them in Cairo and not those Lamptons that used to be in charge and whom everyone disliked so intensely.

Sex with Strangers

One of British law's most notoriously absurd mistakes turned on the fact that in order to be convicted of burglary, the prosecution had to prove that a certain Mr Collins had not just raped the alleged victim but that he had entered her property as a trespasser. The court's 1972 judgment was delivered by Lord Justice Edmund Davies and begins:

> This is about as extraordinary a case as my brethren and I have ever heard. Stephen Collins was convicted on 29 October 1971 of burglary with intent to commit rape and he was sentenced to 21 months' imprisonment.

155

Let me relate the facts . . . At about two o' clock in the early morning of Saturday, 24 July 1971, a young lady of eighteen went to bed at her mother's home in Colchester. She had spent the evening with her boyfriend. She had taken a certain amount of drink . . . She has the habit of sleeping without wearing night apparel in a bed which is very near the lattice-type window of her room . . . At about 3.30 a.m. she awoke and she then saw in the moonlight a vague form crouched in the open window. She was unable to remember, and this is important, whether the form was on the outside of the window sill or on that part of the sill which was inside the room [*this was crucial to the legal case*]. The young lady then realized several things: first of all that the form in the window was that of a male; secondly that he was a naked male; and thirdly that he was a naked male with an erect penis. She also saw in the moonlight that his hair was blond. She thereupon leapt to the conclusion that her boyfriend, with whom for some time she had been on terms of regular and frequent sexual intimacy, was paying her an ardent nocturnal visit. [*The law report does not record whether he was in the habit of doing this on a regular basis.*] She promptly sat up in bed, and the man descended from the sill and joined her in bed and they had full sexual intercourse. But there was something about him which made her think that things were not as they usually were between her and her boyfriend. The length of his hair, his voice as they had exchanged what was described as 'love talk' and other features led her to the conclusion that somehow there was something different. So she turned on the bedside light, saw that her companion was not her boyfriend and slapped the face of the intruder, who was none other than the appellant [*Collins*]. He said to her, 'Give me a good time tonight', and got hold of her arm, but she bit him and told him to go. She then went into the bathroom and he promptly vanished.

The alleged victim in the case was absolutely adamant that had she known that Collins was not her boyfriend she would not have had sex with him. There was, however, no suggestion of any force being used. The judgment continues:

[*Collins*] went on to say that he knew the complainant because he had worked around her house. On this occasion, desiring sexual intercourse . . . he walked around the house, saw a light in an upstairs bedroom, and he knew that this was the girl's bedroom. He found a step ladder, leaned it against the wall and climbed up and looked into the bedroom. What he could see inside through the wide open window was a girl who was naked and asleep. So he descended the ladder and stripped off all his clothes, with the exception of his socks, because apparently he took the view that if the girl's mother entered the bedroom it would be easier to effect a rapid escape if he had his socks on than if he was in his bare feet. That is a matter about which we are not called on to express any view and would in any event find ourselves unable to express one. Having undressed, he then climbed the ladder and pulled himself up on to the window sill. His version of the matter is that he was pulling himself in when she awoke. She then got up and knelt on the bed, she put her arms around his neck and body and she seemed to pull him into the bed. He went on: 'I was rather dazed, because I didn't think she would want to know me. We kissed and cuddled for about ten or fifteen minutes and then I had it away with her but

found it hard because I had had so much to drink' . . .
Now, one feature of the case which remained at the
conclusion of the evidence in great obscurity is where
exactly the appellant was at the moment when,
according to him, the girl manifested that she was
welcoming him. Was he kneeling on the sill outside the
window or was he already inside the room, having
climbed through the window frame, and kneeling on
the inner sill, thereby having committed the trespass
prior to her welcoming invitation?

Unless the jury were entirely satisfied that the appellant made an effective and substantial entry into the
bedroom without the complainant doing or saying
anything to cause him to believe that she was
consenting to his entering it, he ought not to be
convicted of the offence charged.

Eventually, after much judicial consideration, it was felt
that it could not be established that any part of Collins's
body had entered the room uninvited before the alleged
victim invited him in herself. Collins, who therefore had his
conviction quashed, must have considered himself a very
fortunate man indeed.

Bad King James

One afternoon King James VI of Scotland, later to become
King James I of England, was out hunting near Perth, when
his friend Alexander Ruthven, a beautiful boy and the
brother of the much-loved Earl of Gowrie, rode up to him
and asked him over for supper in Gowrie's castle nearby.
After some hemming and hawing, the King, who liked the
company of beautiful boys, agreed and Alexander rode off
home to make preparations.

The King duly arrived at Gowrie's castle with a small company of men and was given a modest supper – due to the lack of time for preparation. According to some reports the Earl of Gowrie behaved rather strangely at supper and didn't spend as much time talking to the King as he ought to have. The King, at least, was keen to tell everyone that the Earl had behaved strangely.

Just as the meal was ending, young Alexander and the King went off together to an upper room in the castle where – according to the King – Ruthven promised to introduce the King to a Jesuit spy he had caught that afternoon. About half an hour into the enquiry, which, for reasons best known to the King, involved him and Ruthven being locked by themselves in a room containing nothing but a bed, a number of people in the street below the bedroom window heard a loud hullabaloo emanating from the chamber in which they knew the King was conducting a special, private investigation. Worried for their monarch's safety, they quickly alerted the King's soldiers who rushed up to the room and found James and Alexander on their own, apparently wrestling. Alexander was immediately killed by the guards.

The Earl of Gowrie ran to the bedroom to discover his brother dead on the floor. King James immediately claimed that the two men had plotted to kill him and that he had somehow miraculously escaped the effects of treason – well, what else could he say? – and Gowrie too was instantaneously executed.

A huge number of influential people all over Europe didn't believe the King, who immediately started ferreting around for evidence to incriminate the Earl and his brother. Not a single person could be found to give evidence against the young nobles, and there was a storm of protest. According to the brutal custom of the time, the corpses of the brothers were taken to Edinburgh and subjected to the

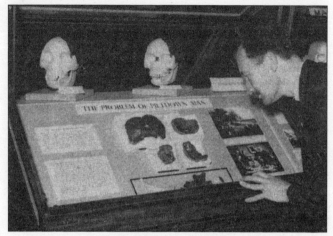

The problems of Piltdown Man

pantomime of a trial. In October (when they had already been dead for ten weeks in midsummer) the rotting bodies were hanged, drawn and quartered and their heads were stuck on poles above Cowgate in Edinburgh.

None of this prevented James succeeding to the English throne just three years later.

Piltdown Man

In 1913 Charles Dawson, a solicitor and amateur anthropologist, was digging about in a gravel pit in Sussex when he came across the skull fragments and bones of a creature which looked remarkably human. He published his findings in the *Quarterly Journal of the Geological Society of London* claiming that, at last, here was the incontrovertible evidence for Charles Darwin's theory of evolution – he had discovered the remains of the missing link in the evolutionary chain between ape and man. It was remarkably fortunate for believers in the Empire that the earliest man just happened to be British. The reconstructed skull was named Eoanthropus Dawsoni as a tribute to the man who found it and the whole scientific world was abuzz with the news.

Meanwhile back in Piltdown, the closest village to the site of the gravel pit in which the bones were found, all sorts of things were happening. The town had become a tourist attraction and coachloads of eminent scientists were to be seen wandering around the area and checking out the site. Further evidence was found to support the original claim and the bones were given to the British Museum who were just thrilled at their own importance and sent copies of the bones to museums all over the world. Piltdown Man had a place in history.

Years later, when dating techniques had improved beyond recognition, the bones were re-examined and discovered to be not 500,000 years old, as Charles Dawson had believed, but a mere 50,000. Piltdown Man's teeth were twentieth-century and, rather more drastically, not actually human at all but those of an orang-utan.

Maiden Voyage

On 28 November 1720 a court in London was called to pass sentence on a large number of pirates who had all been captured in Jamaica. A certain Lieutenant Barret testified that he had caught the whole band of brigands by boarding their boat off the north coast of the island and they had been so unprofessionally drunk that they had all, except two, offered no resistance.

The whole crew were thus hauled to London in chains, the two who had put up a fight being most securely manacled. One of the two had even fired a shot at members of his own crew, enraged at their lack of masculinity in the face of adversity. All the other sailors had conceded defeat meekly, most being incapable of coherent speech.

The death sentence was declared on every single member of the crew and the court went through the ritual of asking if anyone knew of a good reason why this should not be carried out. Normally this question was met with stony silence. On this occasion, however, the two boisterous young lads who had been the only ones to offer resistance called out the age-old expression 'Milord, we plead our bellies'. This was greeted with hoots of derisory laughter since it was the phrase used by young ladies to indicate that they were pregnant and thus could not be hanged. Everyone in the tribunal naturally considered that this was part of the general ribald exchange for which pirates were notorious and carried on laughing but the sailors would not give up. Eventually a court physician was called in to examine the two young men. He came back to the court to announce to a stunned audience and even more stunned crew that the two young men were, in fact, two young women and both were pregnant. The two women, whose stories are now well-known, were called Ann Bonny and Mary Read and both had succeeded in being mistaken for men over an admirably long period of time.

Ann Bonny was apparently the daughter of a serving maid and a married solicitor, born in the Irish town of Kinsale. The affair between her parents caused such a scandal that the two fled Ireland, her father leaving behind him a wife, two children and a hitherto highly respectable practice.

They set up home in Carolina and within a few years Ann's father had become a wealthy man. Ann's mother died and Ann became a potentially very wealthy and therefore much wooed inheritress. She appears to have been unusually independent for someone of her times. On one occasion an ardent fan received nothing for his flirtatious pains save a good, sound thrashing. Very shortly after this Ann eloped with an apparently unemployed sailor called James Bonny and the two of them went to live on the romantically outlawed colony of New Providence in the Bahamas, which had been set up by the legendary Captain Woodes Rogers.

James Bonny turned out to be such a total waste of space that he was not only a good-for-nothing sailor but an even worse outlaw. He betrayed every pirate he came across to the authorities and thus sustained the intense dislike of everyone on the island but particlarly that of his wife.

A proper pirate turned up on the island and immediately captured the romantic imagination of Ann Bonny and she decided to marry him instead. To be fair to the couple, and to Ann's genteel upbringing, they did try to get what was known as a divorce by sale from her first husband. This was a process where, by mutual consent, a wife could be transferred by bill of sale from one man to another. Bonny, true to form, betrayed both of them to the governor of the islands and thus forced the couple to effect a daring escape and head for the open seas. Ann dressed up in seaman's clothes and, together, the pair overpowered the night-watchman at the harbour, stole his boat and set off to sea to join the most notorious boat on the waves, *Haman's Sloop*. Extraordinarily Rackam was the only man on board who knew that Ann was a woman, even when she, apparently, had to be set ashore in Cuba in order to give birth to their first child.

Ann was clearly a woman of spirit. A little while after the birth of her first child a new sailor appeared on board and Ann was seriously attracted to him. She had to be very careful about revealing her secet but, eventually, no longer being able to control her lovelorn passion, she took the young man aside and declared her undying love. Much to her astonishment, the young man took off his hat to reveal his luscious long tresses – he was a she and she was called Mary Read. Rackam, who had been watching his wife with jealous intensity, leapt out from behind the mainsail in an insane fury and accosted the two women. They therefore had no choice but to share their secret with him. Mary Read's story appears to have been even more complicated than Ann's but she also appeared to have a husband on board who was even more spineless than Ann's. Mary had apparently already saved her husband from death by fighting a duel on his behalf and winning.

These bizarre anecdotes saved the two women from the gallows and instead they were no doubt thrilled to be sentenced to life. Mary Read died in childbirth in prison but Ann Bonny survived and, apparently, several of her father's former friends turned up to bail her out and took her back to Jamaica where she lived for many years in peaceful retirement.

Mouth-Organ Man

On one occasion the humorous magazine *Punch* received a long and not particularly funny story from Larry Adler, the harmonica player and broadcaster, in New York. They were undergoing a difficult spell financially and considered themselves very fortunate that anyone famous had bothered to send them a piece at all.

The story was not only unfunny but also remarkably badly written. The senior editor spent a great number of man-hours fiddling about with the sentence structure, rewriting the words and changing the grammar and spelling. Eventually the piece was readable and breathing a sigh of relief, the editor printed it proudly in the next issue of his illustrious but failing magazine.

Almost immediately another complete manuscript arrived from New York. This time the accompanying note was just a little bit longer than the first had been. 'I am so very glad that you used my first story,' proclaimed the writer. Since it had been so well received he thought that the editorial staff might like to know a little bit more about him. He was a nineteen-year-old student at Columbia University who happened to share a name with a world-famous harmonica player.

Ghostblaster

It was 1803 and the citizens of Hammersmith were all very worried. One of the local residents had recently been brutally murdered and the body had been recovered with the throat violently slit. They were convinced that the spirit of the murdered man was roaming along the banks of the River Thames, a ghost of his former self. Tales abounded of sightings of the terrifying white monster with its horns and its howling shrieks. One woman went out for a walk, caught sight of the dreaded creature and instantaneously died of fright.

Two locals, Mr Smith, a highly respected customs officer, and his friend Mr Girdler, the neighbourhood watchman, were determined to form a vigilante group and rid their streets of this terrible threat. Mr Thomas Millwood was a bricklayer. On the evening of 3 January 1804 he went to visit his parents, who happened to live in Hammersmith, on his way home from work. By the time he left it was quite late and he was still wearing his normal work uniform which consisted of long white trousers and a white shirt. Mr Smith and Mr Girdler were on their night-watch when they caught sight of a ghostly white spectre ambling slowly along the banks of the Thames. They immediately concluded that this must be their prey and challenged the ghost to fight them. Being a peaceable soul, mistakenly assuming that he had just encountered two drunken men also on their way home, Mr Millwood decided to turn the other cheek and, ignoring their shouts, he walked on. Mr Smith panicked and shot Mr Millwood who collapsed dead in front of him. Seeing the blood, Mr Smith immediately realized his terrible mistake and surrendered himself to a passing wine merchant.

A mere ten days later he was up in the dock at the Old Bailey accused of murder. Many of the good citizens of Hammersmith came to give evidence about the terrifying reputation of the ghost. Mr Girdler told the jury at great length that Mr Smith was a generous and kind man and one of the best friends he had ever had. Mr Smith himself made a short but moving speech explaining that, whatever he had done, he had done it with the interests of his beloved Hammersmith at heart. The judge, in his summing up, explained to the jury that if they were satisfied that Mr Smith had shot the victim intentionally then he was guilty and there was no defence which could save him. He mistakenly ignored the possibility that Mr Smith might have had the intention to shoot a ghost but certainly not a man. The jury had no choice but to convict. The accused was sentenced immediately to death on the following Monday with his body to be given to surgeons for medical experiments.

Fortunately for Mr Smith a pardon arrived in the nick of time. But the bricklayers of Hammersmith were thereafter very careful always to change into their own clothes before they went home from work.

Ich Bin Ein Berliner

During the Second World War Irving Berlin, the composer, had a massive smash hit with 'White Christmas'. It was considered a tremendous morale boost for Allies everywhere. To celebrate he made a short trip to Britain.

One of Winston Churchill's aides noticed that Mr I. Berlin had arrived in the country and pointed out this heartening fact to the Prime Minister, who was rather too busy to follow current trends in popular culture. The aide was thus surprised at the alacrity with which Churchill sprang into the air and positively urged him to invite the man to a special reception.

Irving Berlin was honoured and flattered to be considered a man of such importance. He was frankly astonished on going in to dinner to be seated right next to the great leader. He was interested in current affairs but he realized that he was a little out of his league on this occasion.

Churchill turned to him with a great air of concentration and leaning forward over the soup, he said:

'So tell me, Mr Berlin, how do you think the war is going?' Irving was thrown. He didn't really feel in a position to respond; he really wasn't able.

'Come now,' said Churchill, 'a man of your stature. No false modesty here. Now tell me, if you were me, what would your next step be?'

Mr Berlin was silenced. He was at a loss for words. He raced his way through the remaining courses, desperately hoping that no one would notice his presence or ask him for an analysis of current military matters, about which he knew no more than the average popular music composer.

After the meal all of the guests departed. Winston Churchill turned around to his wife and his aide and remarked that the Berlin fellow was a remarkably thoughtful chap, terribly natural and unpompous given that he was one of the world's leading philosophical thinkers. His enthusiasm for his dinner guest had been fired by the wrong first name – not knowing anything about white Christmases, he had assumed that I. Berlin was Isaiah Berlin, the philosopher. Mrs Churchill thought it was all very amusing.

Knocking Shop

Elizabethan theatres were places of sex and scandal. The actors, who were always either men or boys, were therefore very keen to make time for interacting with members of the opposite sex at any available opportunity. Richard Burbage, who was Shakespeare's star actor, and generally considered to be a pretty damn sexy fellow, used to arrange assignations while he was performing on stage. On one occasion, he managed to nip out in the interval of *Richard III*, in which he was playing the king, in order to experience a rendezvous with a particularly enthusiastic member of the audience.

Richard, who was naturally in a bit of a hurry, was surprised to find his way barred by an embarrassed servant, furtively guarding the door. The fan, it appeared, was already inside, pursing her devotion with the Bard himself. Richard was furious at being so humbled and banged on the door loudly. Eventually Shakespeare, who was getting fed up with the interruption, sent down a note which bore the message 'William the Conqueror comes before Richard III'. The anonymous fan either didn't notice or didn't care.

Art Botch

Dr Abraham Bredius, a Dutch art historian, was very boastful about his expertise in the seventeenth-century artist, Vermeer. In 1938, he discovered a new painting by his hero called *The Disciples on the Road to Emmaus,* which was immediately bought by the famous Boymans Museum in Rotterdam for the huge sum of £58,000.

Unfortunately, *The Disciples* was actually the work of Hans van Meegeren, an art student, who had specifically painted the picture to expose Bredius and the art cognoscenti in The Netherlands. Bredius was later taken in by ten other paintings by van Meegeren and the fraud was only discovered when the latter owned up to selling an imitation Vermeer to Goering in 1945 and subsequently confessed all.

Bredius' influence was so powerful that nobody believed van Meegeren until he painted another Vermeer, *Jesus and the Scribes,* under their very noses.

Christopher Columbus

Born in 1451 in the Italian port of Genoa, Christopher Columbus was attracted to water. He went to sea as a pimpled youth, proceeded to marry the daughter of a Portuguese navigator and settled down happily in Lisbon.

Christopher was very highly influenced by his reading of a fashionable book of the period, Ptolemy's *Geography.* From this work Columbus learnt two main facts: (1) that the world was a perfect sphere (which is clearly a mistake) and (2) that the known world extends in a continuous land-mass from the western extremities of Europe to the easternmost limit of Asia and that between the two ends of this land-mass on the other side of the sphere, there was one single intervening ocean (which was clearly also a mistake). Theoretically, it would thus be possible, according to Ptolemy, to cross from Europe to Asia via the Atlantic Ocean.

Ptolemy also reckoned that the proportions of land to ocean were identical and therefore the Atlantic would be too wide for any vessel in existence at the time to be able to cross it. Columbus didn't like this part of the book so he dismissed it as incorrect.

With the assistance of his brother and expert chart-maker, Bartholomew Columbus, Christopher, a most charming and sophisticated fellow, used the parts of Ptolemy which supported his argument to acquire the support of Ferdinand and Isabella of Spain in his mission to discover the other route to the Indies.

On 3 August 1492, Columbus embarked from the port of Palos in his trusty boat the *Santa Maria* and set sail for a destination due west. On 12 October 1492, after quelling a potential mutiny on board by sheer force of personality, he landed in the Bahamas, believing himself to be in China. He kept notes on the native people, as if he were making notes about the Chinese, and he explored Haiti. He returned to Barcelona to a hero's welcome.

In September 1493, Columbus once again set sail, landing this time in Puerto Rico which he considered to be an island in the Indian Ocean. This is when things began to go badly wrong. A large number of colonizers had sailed with Columbus, thinking that they were about to get rich on gold. Columbus, however, was very keen that they should all plant vegetables. The unhappy Spaniards seized most of the boats and returned to Spain. Those who remained were disgusted to discover that the local food was horrible, the weather was lousy and there wasn't a nugget of gold to be found.

Columbus wasn't a man to be easily deterred by the big things in life. It was during his third voyage to the East Indies that Magellan and Da Gama actually did reach the Orient, thus discrediting Columbus completely whilst he was still claiming that Honduras was, in fact, Japan. Two years later he returned to Spain, a broken man, but still pretty wealthy.

Over 'ere Landlord

The eighteenth-century playwright, Oliver Goldsmith, was riding late in Kent one night, when he lost his way and found himself in a town called Ardagh.

It started to rain, so he stopped a passing fencing master named Kelly and asked him where the best house in the town was to be found, intending to spend the night there. Kelly, who assumed, quite reasonably, that he was enquiring about local architecture, directed him to the splendid and ancient residence of Sir Ralph Featherstone, a local landowner. Goldsmith found the house, blustered in out of the cold and promptly ordered himself a hearty supper. Featherstone himself came downstairs to find out what was going on and Goldsmith warmly invited him and his entire family to join him for a meal. The landowner, an old friend of Goldsmith's family but a stranger to Goldsmith himself, recognized the young writer and decided to play along with the charade.

Goldsmith went on to order two bottles of wine, a bed for the night and a hot bowl of porridge for his breakfast before he tried to pay his bill and discovered his error. This incident is said to have inspired his most famous play *She Stoops to Conquer*.

Nixon Likes Jazz

In 1971, the White House threw a birthday party for the bandleader Duke Ellington. The great Cab Calloway was one of the guests and he was a bit shy of the grandness of the occasion and so stood quietly waiting his turn in the receiving line. To his surprise, President Nixon strode straight over to him and pumped his hand so warmly that Calloway thought he must be a special fan. 'Pat and I love your music,' crooned the President, 'and it's a great honour to have you here. Happy Birthday, Mr Ellington.'

Son of God

Sabbatai Zevi, who was born and brought up in Smyrna, was a Jew who considered, for reasons best known to himself, that he was the Messiah. From 1651 until 1665 he travelled around the large Jewish communities of the Middle East claiming not only that he was the Messiah but also that he would usher in the millennium quite specifically in the year 1666. By 1665 he had convinced a large number of other people of this notion and his disciples spread the word with great enthusiasm to many others.

By the time he returned to his native Smyrna in 1665 he received a hero's welcome. Everyone went mad. All the natives prepared for a speedy exodus to the Holy Land, considering that the Age of the Messiah was about to descend upon them. Businessmen everywhere were so sure of the correctness of their facts that they neglected their trade and began to sell up, in preparation for the imminent return to Jerusalem.

A necessary first step to the Age of the Messiah was that the Sultan of the Ottoman Empire had to be deposed. Following this simple logic, and knowing that they could not fail, Sabbatai and his followers all landed on the Dardanelle coast early in 1666 and were promptly arrested by local policemen and dragged to Constantinople in chains and pitiful ignominy.

This did not, however, dampen the ardour of his followers who decided that the fact that he had not been massacred straight away was even clearer proof that he must be the true Messiah. A constant procession of adoring visitors streamed through the prison in Constantinople where Sabbatai played it up no end and continued to disseminate tales of his miraculous endeavours.

Contemporary reports indicate that in large commercial towns all over Europe, where the Jews led the business world, stagnation of trade took a terrible toll on all local enterprise. Citizens everywhere packed up their linen and their dry goods in order to prepare for the imminent journey home.

The Sultan had to think up a sophisticated way of coping with the problem without making Sabbatai into an instant martyr. He thus attempted to convert Sabbatai to Islam. Almost immediately the plan worked. Curiously many of his original followers could not accept Sabbatai's mistake and resolved it in their own minds by continuing to pursue their original conviction with a somewhat muddled vigour. They also converted in their hundreds.

Nazi View

'Christ cannot possibly have been a Jew. I don't have to prove that scientifically. It's a fact!' said Joseph Goebbels.

Bonking in the Bois de Boulogne

Famous men have always held a certain allure for members of the public and, according to contemporary and highly scandalized local newspaper reports, Anatole France, the nineteenth-century French philosopher and novelist, was no exception. On one memorable occasion he was noisily engaged in sexual activity with a somewhat recalcitrant girl-friend in the main Parisian park, the Bois de Boulogne, when an enthusiastic and moustachioed gendarme leapt out from behind one of the other bushes in a state of some agitation.

'Sir,' he exclaimed, 'your behaviour is reprehensible and, indeed, highly detrimental to the moral conduct of all local children. I beg you and your lady friend to desist immediately or I shall be forced to arrest you, Sir, with or without your clothes.'

France sat upright and drew out from within his jacket pocket a visiting card which he showed to the gendarme, who was immediately contrite.

'Oh Sir, I'm so terribly sorry, Sir, I had no idea that you were a member of the Académie Française. Pray forgive me, Sir. I couldn't possibly be expected to guess. All kinds of unsuitable people come to have sex here. Had I known I wouldn't have dreamt of bothering you.'

The recalcitrant ladyfriend was thrilled since she had not known that her partner was a celebrity. They went back into the bush and continued to disturb its roots with great vigour.

Chapter Eleven

Inattention to Detail

In one of the London County Courts a barrister, who appeared to be rather tense and nervous, called his first witness into the box. After the witness had sworn the oath, the barrister went through the normal court procedure of asking him to verify his name and address.

'Is it correct,' he said, 'that your name is Mr Bumbum Fricks?'

'Why no!' exclaimed the irate witness, who was considerably put out by this violent insult to his person. 'My name is Mr Bumbum and I am a Fellow of the Royal Institute of Chartered Surveyors.'

In Preston Crown Court in November 1983 a man accused of the theft of a large amount of jewellery was in mid-trial. His defence was mistaken identity. He wasn't there, didn't know anything about it and it wasn't him. As the Prosecuting Counsel Peter Oppenshaw began his cross-examination of the defendant, a large commotion was heard at the back of the courtroom. The defendant's wife had just walked in with several of her friends.

Suddenly one of the victims of the burglary began to shriek hysterically. The wife of the accused had turned up at court wearing most of the victim's family heirlooms. Mr Oppenshaw turned slowly to the jury and, savouring the moment for all it was worth, he declared:

'Ladies and gentlemen, I am sure you will agree that this turn of events has given the accused's line of defence something of a hollow ring.'

Weird News Stories

Miss Fiona Gordon, nine years old, went on an educational trip to her local museum in County Durham in 1971. Here she came across one of the star exhibits of the collection: a coin labelled very carefully with the notation 'Roman AD 135'.

Miss Gordon, a remarkable primary school student, immediately pointed out to one of the museum attendants that the labelling on the coin was, in fact, almost 2,000 years out. She recognized the object straight away, she said, as the kind of plastic token that was supplied as a free gift when you collected a certain number of the requisite bottle labels. She had known instantaneously that this was the case since the supplier's distinctive logo was printed on the exhibit.

A curator at the museum explained that labelling difficulties had arisen because the logo consisted of a rather individual capital R, which the scientific team had considered to stand for 'Made in Rome', when really it meant 'Robinson's', the lemon barley people.

A dummy hanging by a noose at the Long Beach Amusement Park in California formed part of a 'fun house' exhibit in the centre for over five years.

It was such a convincing piece that it was often used as a prop for films which were being shot in the Park. During the filming of an episode of *The Six Million Dollar Man*, one of the film cameramen became dissatisfied with the way in which the right arm was hanging from the body of the dummy and was attempting to adjust it in order to make it look real when the whole arm fell off. On closer examination a protruding bone was noted and he identified the dummy as a human corpse.

Authorities described the corpse as an elderly man of five foot three but could not tell when he had actually died. The figure, wrapped in gauze and sprayed with fluorescent paint, had been bought by the amusement park from a local wax museum.

It used to be a very commonly held misconception that toads secrete a deadly venom. The husband of an Italian woman was dying of dropsy, but taking far too long over the business for her liking. She accordingly procured a toad and put it into his wine so that he might drink the liquid and die. Instead, and much to her astonishment, he completely recovered overnight.

As everyone knows, toad venom is the single best cure for dropsy.

Anthony Daniels of Enfield in north London thought that his career was made when he gained control of a takeaway food outlet in the centre of London. He took control of every aspect of his new business – staff, fresh produce, attractive decor – but one small oversight led to humiliation.

One April evening in 1993 Ms Pothecary, a suitably named nurse, visited 'Anthony's Takeaway' in the West End and purchased a salad which she carried home and ate. She was chewing through the final morsel when her jaws came to rest against what she believed to be a lump of poorly shredded cabbage. It resisted her attempts to ingest it and so she spat it out and had a quick look. She realized almost immediately that it was the top of someone's thumb complete with thumbnail still intact.

Ms Fothecary put the thumb in the fridge overnight and the next morning marched down to the Camden Environmental Health Department, bearing the digit angrily before her.

Two days later, an official from the council went to investigate at 'Anthony's' and found Mr Campos, the cook, busy chopping away, his right hand swathed in bandages.

Weird News Stories

Anthony Daniels was called to the scene. Mr Campos had been shredding cabbage, he explained on behalf of his employee, when he cut off half his thumb and was rushed to hospital. Another employee finished making up the salads but Mr Daniels completely forgot that one crucial detail – the whereabouts of the missing digit.

Mr Daniels, who blamed this mistake on the stupidity of his colleagues, was fined £200. Ms Pothecary was awarded an extra £200 for shock to the system.

In 1906 an excellent chemical called sulfanilamide was discovered which was most efficacious in the treatment of blood poisoning. One US drug company named Massengill cashed in on the discovery by launching a pink raspberry-flavoured medicine called 'Elixir of Sulfanilamide'. It sold like hot cakes. Unfortunately they decided to dissolve the magical chemical in the deadly poison diethylene glycol and at least 107 people died of kidney failure after taking it. The chemist who had developed the drug died too, by committing suicide.

A New York bank computer programmer realized in 1970 that if he stole a few cents each month from all the customers in his bank he would become very rich without anyone noticing. In order to do this, he wrote a program that rounded everyone's balance down to the nearest ten cents each month and transferred the balance into the account of whichever name was last in the alphabetical list of account holders. He then opened an account for himself in the name of A Zyglit (an anagram of Lazy Git) and settled down happily to become a millionaire.

Things went wrong for the fraudster when a Polish immigrant named Zyzov moved into the neighbourhood and opened an account at the same bank. After a couple of months he politely wrote to the bank to ask why they appeared to be paying such enormous interest on his very small savings. The whole sham was discovered and the programmer was sent down for a number of years. If only he had called himself Zyzyzyk.

The most famous of all inefficient phrase books is the English–Portuguese one devised by the inimitable Pedro Carolino, who in 1883 created *The New Guide of the Conversation in Portuguese and English*. Mr Carolino, who had little, if any, grasp of our native tongue, was suitably ill-equipped for the linguistic task he had so bravely set himself. Armed only with a Portuguese–French dictionary and a French–English dictionary he set about his guide to the English language by cross-referencing the two, not wishing to confuse matters by testing out the results on any English speakers. This intriguing methodology led to the kind of marvellously spontaneous-sounding language he employs in his opening sentences:

'We expect then, who the little book (for the care what we wrote him, and for her typographical correction) that may be worth the accept ation of the studious persons, and expecially of the youth, at which we dedicate him particularly.'

This intriguing introduction is followed by a section entitled 'Familiar Phrases' which includes such topical tips as 'Have you say that?', 'Exculpate me by your brother's', 'These apricots and these peaches make me to come water in mouth' and that particularly familiar phrase 'He laughs at my nose, he jest by me'. This chapter is concluded with the words 'End First Part's to be followed by familiar dialogues'. These, too, are particularly useful. You could greet your new English friends with the words 'For to wish the good morning' and you could leave them with the parting shot 'Adieu my dear. I leave you. If can to see you at six clock to the hotel, we swill dive together willingly'.

Helpfully, he offers some good words of advice for exchanging with your local barber:

'Comb me quick; don't put so much pomatum. What news tell me? All hairs dresser are newsmonger.'

He continues with a section entitled aptly 'Idiotisms and Proverbs' and these include all of your regulars: 'He sin in troubled water', 'To look for a needle in a hay bundle' not to forget that old chestnut 'It want to beat the iron during it is hot'.

Finally, Carolino offers some chatty little anecdotes with which to entertain new friends:

'One eyed was laied against a man which had good eyes that he saw better than him. The party was accepted. I had gain, over said the one eyed; why I se you two eyes, and you not look me who one.'

Carolino considered that this phrase was guaranteed to give any London girl on the lookout for a hot night on the town something to reckon with. And who can blame him?

During the 1820s Mr Justice Graham was famed as the politest judge at the Old Bailey. He was extremely courteous at all times. On one occasion sixteen defendants appeared before him accused of petty theft. Mistakenly Mr Graham read out only fifteen of the sixteen names on the indictment before him and sentenced every single one of the fifteen to death. Glumly, the fifteen men trod their weary way back to the cell in which they would await the gallows.

The sixteenth man whose name had been left off the death list, breathed a sigh of enormous relief. The Clerk of the Court caught sight of him and turned to address the judge. What was to be done with the man whom he had quite mistakenly saved? Mr Justice Graham politely enquired after the gentleman's name and was told by his Clerk that it was John Robins.

'Oh Mr Robins,' said the judge in his most deferential way, 'I am terribly sorry for the inconvenience I have caused you. I find that I have quite by accident left your name from the list of people doomed to death. It was quite accidental I assure you and I beg your pardon for my mistake. I am truly sorry and can only add to my profound apologies the fact that you will be hanged tomorrow with the rest of them.'

In 1887 *The Times* published a series of articles which were intended to show that Charles Parnell, the leading Irish nationalist, was an extremely dangerous political agitator. One of the main pieces of evidence used to back up this claim was a letter, supposedly written by Parnell himself, which expressed total support for the murder of the English under-secretary of Ireland by a Republican terrorist. Parnell immediately made a public statement to the effect that the letter was a forgery and, indeed, that he even knew the identity of the forger, one Richard Pigott.

Pigott was charged and Parnell was represented by the leading barrister of his day, Sir Charles Russell. Russell had looked through all of the apparently forged letters very thoroughly indeed. He had paid particular attention to any idiosyncratic spelling mistakes, the most notable of which was the misspelling of the word 'hesitancy'.

The first few days of the trial had gone very well for Pigott and he had not made a single mistake. Two days into cross-examination Pigott was blooming with over-confidence, which Russell, an experienced observer of men, could tell immediately. Russell had a piece of paper handed up to Pigott and asked him to write some words down on it, inferring that the whole purpose was to have examples of Pigott's handwriting. First Pigott spelt out the word 'livelihood' as requested. Then he was asked to write the word 'likelihood'. A little later Pigott was asked to sign his name and then, finally, almost as an afterthought, Russell mentioned the word 'hesitancy'. Things were going swimmingly and Pigott was only too happy to oblige. He picked up the pen and immediately and mistakenly wrote the word 'hesitency'. He was doomed. By the following morning he had fled to Paris where he wrote a signed confession and, within the month, he had shot himself dead.

On 28 July 1962 the Mariner I space probe was launched from Cape Canaveral headed directly for Venus. Never before had this been attempted in so technical a way. The craft would cruise at over 25,000 miles an hour and in only 100 days Mariner would be circling the great planet with the mysterious cloudy rings.

A mere four minutes after take-off Mariner I hurled headlong downwards and straight into the Atlantic Ocean. A subsequent inquiry revealed that the cause of this accident was the absence of a minus sign which had, unfortunately, been omitted from the computer program. This oversight was a result of human error and cost NASA a staggering £4,280,000.

One dull afternoon in Reno in 1983, Eddie Blake decided to have a go at robbing a bank. 'This is a hold-up,' declared the note that he handed to the woman behind the counter, 'put all the money into a bag and hand it over.' Within seconds he was clutching the loot and running for it.

By the time he got home, the police were waiting outside his door to arrest him. He had scrawled the demand note on the back of one of his business cards. It contained his name, address and telephone number.

Clive Castro of Cooperville, Texas, did manage to get safely out of the bank that he had just robbed. He dived into the nearest passenger car, shouting, 'Drive off, buster, and make it snappy.' The driver made it very snappy indeed. Castro had run into a patrol car which drove him straight to the nearest police station.

Javiar Ortiz, aged twenty-five, of Badajoz, Spain was a higher grade of criminal altogether. For one thing, he realized that the last place to go after a bank raid was home. For sophisticated technical reasons which are not entirely clear to the non-criminal mind, he decided that it would be a great idea to run into the nearest convent and dress up as a nun.

His first mistake was that he became hungry and stole down to the kitchen where he stole a leg of ham which he stuck up his habit. The Mother Superior walked past at this moment and was fairly sure that her convent did not contain any pregnant nuns. His second mistake was that although he was wearing full religious regalia he had not bothered to change out of his size ten Wellington boots. This convinced the Mother Superior of his fake identity. She blew her whistle and twenty eager nuns suddenly surrounded him, separated him from his unsightly habit and turned him over to an astonished local police force.

For over a quarter of a century John Bratby, the painter, was married to a lady called Jean Cooke. Eventually the pair got divorced and some time after that Bratby got remarried to another lady who was called Patricia.

At the register office, the registrar reached the point in the ceremony at which the ring was required. Patricia turned around to Bratby and asked him to ask the best man for the ring. Following years of domestic ritual Bratby replied, without a moment's hesitation.

'Yes of course, Jean.'

John Haigh taunted police in London with the idea that he

had murdered a rich widow called Mrs Olive Durand-Deacon. When they came to arrest him, he laughed and declared that he had destroyed the body with acid and that, although they would find the sludge in the garden of her house, every trace of identification would now have disappeared.

The police sent a pathologist called Keith Simpson to dig about in the bushes. First he found a gallstone and then, even worse, Mrs Durand-Deacon's acrylic dentures. John Haigh was hanged at Wandsworth prison on 10 August 1949. If he had waited three more weeks to boast about his success, the disintegration of the body would have been complete.